# Ready-to-use Layouts

## *for Desktop Design*

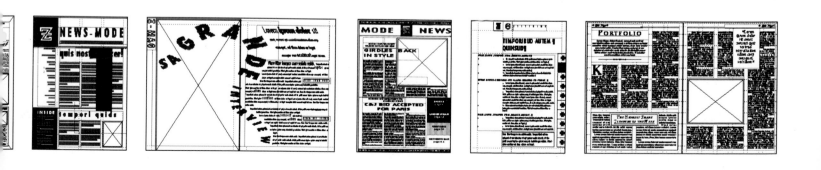

1995

Nam liber tempor
cum soluta nobis.
Autem sud

Ullam corp
relillum et aur.

THE INVESTOR

# Ready-to-use Layouts

# for *Desktop Design*

David Collier and Kay Floyd

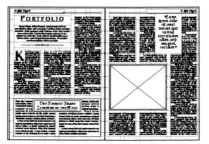

**NORTH LIGHT BOOKS**

Cincinnati, Ohio

**A QUARTO BOOK**

Copyright ©1989 Quarto Publishing plc

First published in the USA by
North Light Books, an imprint of
F&W Publications, Inc
1507 Dana Avenue
Cincinnati, Ohio 45207: (800) 289-0963

ISBN  0 89134 287 7

Reprinted 1995

**This book was designed and produced by**
Quarto Publishing plc
The Old Brewery
6 Blundell Street
London N7 9BH

**Senior Editor** Susanna Clarke

**Editor** Neelam Sharma

**Designer** David Collier

**Art Director** Moira Clinch
**Editorial Director** Carolyn King

**Imagesetting** by Laserbureau, London W1
**Manufactured** in Hong Kong By Regent Publishing Services Ltd
**Printed** in China by Leefung-Asco Printers Ltd.

**Special thanks to**
Andy Benedek and Sue Wadham of TransType, Essendon,
Joe Gillespie of Pixel Productions,
Jan Pelczynski, Nick Franchini and Nico Macdonald at DeCode Design.

# About this book:

Practice what you preach.

This book was produced using a desktop publishing system.

**The first stage** was to produce the layouts to be featured and illustrated. All of these were first designed as thumbnails, using a pen and paper, and then worked out on the computer. It is still quicker to use a pen to do very rough roughs than to work up ideas to a finished state on the computer.

The final layouts were produced using a variety of packages including Illustrator, FreeHand, PageMaker, Quark XPress, Microsoft Word, LetraStudio, and MacPaint.

These layouts were printed on a laserprinter and approved by the publisher. The captions were then written on another computer system, using a word-processing program, and given to the designer on disk.

The designer then turned this text into typesetting-quality text, changing all straight, word-processed quotation marks, and apostrophes ( " " and ' ) into typographically correct "curly" quotation marks ( " " and '). Double spaces after periods were changed into single spaces, and dashes, which in the word-processed text appeared as hyphens, were changed to em or en dashes.

**The next step** involved making up the final page artworks of the book and plugging the caption text into the correct pages. Great care was taken in setting up a default page that contained all the necessary boxes for page numbers, introduction paragraphs, and style sheets.

Because the page makeup package used did not allow graphic elements to bleed across pages, it was decided to do page artworks as "spreads" – i.e., one page on the computer would correspond to two pages of the book. This made auto page-numbering impossible, but enabled thumbnails to be more easily printed.

To insure the captions aligned with the correct items in the layouts, "screen-dumps" were placed in position on the page artworks. (A screen dump is literally a snapshot of the screen. However, it contains none of the high-resolution PostScript information needed to print a page of good typographical quality, but it is adequate as a position guide – much like a conventional blue keyline). Drop-shadows were also put on the illustrations at this point. A 90-line screen was used, as the printer would be shooting these complicated screens from bromide, and finer screens tend to fill in when reshot.

Cropmarks were drawn on the computer pages rather than relying on the software's built-in crop-mark generation, so page folds could be accurately indicated.

Because the captions are often set across a very small width, hyphenation was turned off on the majority of pages, but all the spreads containing chunks of text were done as separate documents with auto-hyphenation switched on.

**When corrected and approved**, the completed artworks were sent to a typesetting house to be output on a high-resolution typesetter.

**The final stage** was for the printer to shoot the layouts at the correct size and drop them into the correct keyline holes left on the page artworks of the book. This could have been done on the computer but would not have been time- and cost-effective because of the complications involved in reducing elements in the layouts to many different sizes.

Color proofs were returned and corrected and the book printed and distributed.

# Contents

Desktop publishing is widely acknowledged as a method of producing publications which requires three distinct skills: computer operation, editorial, and design.

Whereas computer operation is a skill that can be acquired fairly easily, the ability to write and design are much harder to come by.

But not everyone realizes this until they have bought their desktop publishing system. Many believe that simply by purchasing some computer equipment, they can immediately become publishers of successful, well-written, visually appealing magazines, books or newsletters. It is only when they start to use their systems that they find out this is not so. Some of the work that has come from desktop publishing systems in recent times is a testament to this.

During its short history, desktop publishing has changed the way many of the things we read are produced. The dtp "revolution" theoretically allows a single person, perhaps the marketing manager in your company, to become typographer, pasteup artist, editor, writer, compositor and graphic artist – all of which were once specialist skills practiced by people who (a) had the talent, and (b) had years of training and experience behind them. A single, untrained person cannot be expected to acquire and use all these various skills effectively.

But, with the help of the layouts contained in this book, someone with little or no design experience will be able to produce good-looking documents. All these examples were produced on an Apple Macintosh computer and were created using a variety of application packages such as page layout, word processing, draw and paint. Some effects are produced by complicated processes – so you need to have been trained in software techniques and to know your application packages before starting to put these examples into practice.

There are a few basic design rules, most of which have their roots in common sense. For example, a poster or magazine cover is far more likely to attain the successful communication it sets out to achieve if it is both simple and direct. A wall poster gets approximately four seconds' worth of attention paid to it by a passer-by so it has to make an immediate impact if it is to be remembered.

Thus, a magazine cover that is gray with masses of small text, or a poster or handbill which is trying to explain the mysteries of the universe will probably fail in its objective, which is to grab the attention of a potential purchaser or reader.

A magazine has to compete with many others on a newsstand's crowded display in order to gain the attention of the casual buyer. The browser will be attracted by a strong, simple image which has a clear, coherent identity. Only then will the publication be given more than a cursory glance.

A publication is made up of two elements – words and pictures. Let us look closely into the roles played by each of these before we go on to discuss design techniques to show you how to use them to best advantage.

When beginning any design venture, ideas roughed out on paper will help you to visualize and formulate your objectives while taking account of the design parameters of your publication. Even professional designers who now use desktop publishing still take up pen and pencil before committing their ideas to computer screen. Look at the overall shapes you are making with the text, graphics and space. Don't get bogged down with fancy effects. Explore one basic idea and gradually it will become complicated. Now that you are the designer you can fully explore your medium – but you must first consider what you want to express within the strictures of mood and theme.

## Type

The prime function of words is to communicate instantly, and the overuse of fancy typefaces can impair this function. While a difference in type style helps to attract the reader's eye, it is the difference in type size that helps organize information in terms of its relative importance.

The most fundamental distinction between typefaces is whether they are serif or sans serif, and this has an effect on their legibility. Serifs are the "feet" or "arms" on the end of the strokes of some letters and they facilitate reading. The typeface called Times Roman is one of the most popular and common serif typefaces and it is to be found in digitized form in most desktop publishing systems. Serifs are said to help the eye jump from character to character. Given this fact, serif faces are ideal for main text (for

the bulk of type as opposed to headlines) although there is no hard-and-fast rule which says that you cannot use sans serif typefaces for body copy. In fact, they can be used to great effect in certain circumstances, combined with a serif typeface for headlines.

Generally, sans serif typefaces make good headings (as used by popular tabloid newspapers) and, because of their simplicity, they can handle virtually any amount of letterspacing.

Typeface families are available in different thicknesses (called "weights"). A typeface is usually available in light, medium, regular, bold, and extra bold weights.

Each letter in a typeface family is constructed from a combination of pen strokes. The difference between a thin and thick stroke is known as "stress." When two strokes in a letter meet or cross, one stroke will be thick and the other thin. This achieves contrast and therefore clarity and elegance. In very light or very bold typefaces this contrast is lost. But if there is too much contrast between thick and thin the effect can be crude and overpowering.

A bold font is not necessarily more legible than a light one. (A font is a complete set of type in one style and size.) Clarity is achieved not only by the thickness of the strokes, but also by their distance from each other and from the strokes of adjacent letters in the same word. If these strokes are too close together or too far apart, then the reader has problems absorbing the message (take note all desktop publishers who have access to user-defined fonts which can be manipulated to fit the size allocated or who think they are creating some stunning effect by stretching or widening letters).

Typeface fashions come and go. In the 1940s for example, it was de rigueur to use Bodoni as body copy.

For the purpose of clarity and in order not to commit stylistic suicide, it is best to stick to typeface classics such as Times Roman, Helvetica, Bodoni and Century Schoolbook. The first two faces will usually be supplied as standard on good desktop publishing systems and the others can be bought separately on disk and downloaded into your system's hard disk. Although only four faces have been mentioned here, this is usually enough for most publication work. In the early days of desktop publishing, many manufacturers boasted that their software allowed the user to mix and print ten or more styles in one document. In practice, this is an absolute disaster in terms of good typographic design and should be avoided at all costs. As a general rule, two typefaces (a headline face and a body copy face) are adequate for most page designs. A variety of textures and styles can be conveyed by your choice of leading (the white space between the lines of type), typeface weight and size, and by altering the spacing between letters.

Different typefaces have different uses. There are literally thousands of typefaces in use around the world. One supplier, Linotype, has more than 2000 typefaces in its library, although not all these have been digitized for use on a computer. Your desktop publishing system will come with a selection of faces suited to particular tasks. Some will be designed specifically to be legible on a computer screen and therefore are not very effective when used on, say, a legal document. Legibility and overall cleanliness of appearance will be attained with a face such as Times Roman, which is also adequate for use on the screen.

In the layouts in this book we have selected a range of different type styles which we felt were appropriate to the images our fictitious companies wanted to project. ElektroSynth, a manufacturer of electronic music equipment, wants a clean, modern image; Bubbles, a soap manufacturer, wants a mainstream, middle-of-the-road style; Bull & Smith, certified public accountants, need a classic, traditional look; VAC Chemical has a tough, industrial image; and Z-Mode fashion needs to seem young and right at the forefront of design trends.

The companies use appropriate typefaces to produce a variety of published material that reflects their style and corporate identity.

The designer in search of a modern look for text and layout (like ElektroSynth) might consider the following approaches. A "modern" typeface such as Century Schoolbook could be used. ElektroSynth, however, uses an ultra-clean graphic design with a sans serif typeface, Futura. Our examples show Futura condensed, light and extra bold. Some variation has been provided with the sparing use of a distorted Bodoni which has a tiny, hairline serif. These letterforms are matter of fact and clean-cut.

Typefaces which suit the kind of mainstream image our soap manufacturer wants to project include Baskerville, Caslon and Times Roman. Those used in our examples are Souvenir and Cooper, both of which have rounded serifs.

VAC Chemical wants a forceful, but fairly conservative, style. This has been achieved using a bold, sans serif face for headlines (Franklin Gothic Heavy) and, to provide a strong contrast, a serif face (Century Schoolbook) for text. The designer could also have chosen a slab serif face such as Rockwell, Clarendon, Italienne, Egyptian, Italia, Memphis, Prestige Elite or other typewriter faces which you may find on your desktop publishing system. In these faces there is little or no difference between the different strokes. All elements of the letterform, including serifs, have the same optical stroke thickness. This applies both for light as well as heavy weights. Emphasis on serifs is the common stylistic element.

Baskerville and Caslon were used as examples to convey a classic style for our certified public accountants. Others that would help ensure a traditional and "well-established" image for a publication include Garamond and Goudy Old Style. Baskerville, Caslon, and Garamond fall into the group of typefaces generally known as "old style." Old style typefaces were modelled on the writing style called "humanist minuscule." Written with a broadish pen, the humanist minuscule showed very little difference between main strokes and hairlines. The pen was usually held at a 30 degree angle, hence the triangular serifs. This style first appeared around 1470 in Venice. The version that the French punch-cutter, Claude Garamond, made in the sixteenth century, was one of the most expressive examples of an old style face.

Z-Mode, our fashion company, wants to project a contemporary image that appeals to the youth market. This category of typefaces is more difficult to define than the others because, as we have already seen, typeface popularity comes and goes. However, you will see that distortion of type is a repeated feature in the design of Z-Mode's publications and sales material.

## Graphics

The second and equally important element in document design is graphics. A picture is worth a thousand words, so it is said, but it is your job as a designer to balance the words and the pictures to make both equally effective and interesting to the reader.

Graphics which can be used in desktop publishing include photographs (halftones), line art (illustrations such as cartoons), digitized logos, charts and graphs produced with a business graphics software package, and your own illustrations and diagrams produced with a paint or draw software package. Some color work such as photographs and transparencies can be introduced provided you have the right equipment to do so. In this case a color scanner and monitor are required. With packages such as Adobe Illustrator it is now possible for a user to create original color drawings on screen and use these in the publication. It is more usual, though, if you want to include color in your publication just to leave the appropriate space on the layout and have the printer drop the picture into place at a later stage.

This highlights yet another problem which desktop publishing can pose. As we have seen, with the appropriate software, a single person can become writer, editor, designer, pasteup artist and typographer. Now there are software packages that exist to enable the same person to become a cartoonist and illustrator as well. If you are hopeless at drawing, I would advise that you leave these packages to those who have the talent and the time to use them effectively. Alternatively, if you want to use cartoons and illustrations in your publication, but don't have the budget to use a professional illustrator, you could use one of the clip-art packages available. These contain sets of predrawn artwork such as symbols, fancy borders, and cartoon characters (both people and animals) which can be included in your design. Many of the designs contained in the following pages use special effects from the Zapf Dingbats font. This is a set of shapes and symbols, such as stars and hands with a pointing finger (to give a "this way" sign), produced by the German typeface designer, Zapf. It was among the early fonts to be digitized for use on a computer, and so is easily available to desktop publishing users. Predrawn artwork is a valuable asset in the designer's armory and provides instant graphics.

Tints and boxes are a form of graphics that represent an easy way to introduce variety and interest to a page. A monochrome page can be easily enhanced with the use of a 10 or 20 per cent gray tint. Tints can be used effectively on a page that only has text and can highlight logos, headlines and subheads, or be laid over simple graphics.

## Design techniques

We have seen what sort of text and graphics you will use. Now we will look at how to put them together to make a coherent, well-designed page.

One way is to take all your elements, text and graphics, back to the drawing board and design a page, using pencil and paper, that will both be attractive to the reader and convey your main message. You should come away with an overall shape for the page which, hopefully, balances text and illustration, giving an overall pattern of shapes and tones which are in proportion and well balanced. It may help to think of geometric shapes to create the layout. And don't forget the different effects that justified, ranged right or ranged left text will have on the overall look of the page.

The easiest way of achieving proportion and balance is to design your page on a grid. Throughout the following pages various grids have been designed for work published by our companies. For most of their publications, the companies stick to one grid, or house style, to achieve a uniform look. These measurements may be a useful guide that you can use for your own publications.

The overall page depth and width is defined by margins, and within that space, vertical columns determine where text and graphics will be placed. The page depth will depend on the size of type to be used, the leading (space between the lines of type), and the outside margins. As a rough guide, in book work the foot, or bottom, margin should be about twice the size of the head, or top, margin. In magazines, a large top margin is often useful to incorporate section titles such as "News," "Interview," and so on. The fore edge margin (closest to the edge of the paper) is usually an average of the top and bottom margins put together and the back margin (where two pages join in the middle of a spread) should be about half the fore edge. When planning the back margin, take into account the type of binding to be used. Saddle stitching allows more of the back margin to be seen by the reader, perfect binding less (see binding methods below).

The number of columns used on each page can vary. Some desktop publishing systems will allow you to create up to ten columns on a page. This is acceptable for broadsheet publications such as newspapers, but is impractical for smaller documents. Most of these will be laid out to a maximum of four columns per page.

Single-column layouts can be difficult to read because the eye has to follow a long line of words across a wide area, and illustrations and crossheads can be difficult to fit. In this case the method is best suited to small books and pamphlets. However bear in mind that the single column does not have to extend across the whole width of the page and wide margins on both sides of the text, providing a lot of white space, can look very classy.

Two-column layouts are easy to read and allow more flexibility to place graphics, captions and crossheads. Although suited to most types of publication, two-column layouts are most often used in newsletter design.

Three-column layouts give more scope for the designer to use imaginative graphics and are generally used in magazine feature design. A smallish point size of about nine or ten is used here. (Points are the most usual method of typographic measurement. There are 72 points to the inch.) Thinner columns, as used in a four-column grid, create a pacy, less bookish feel. They are often used for magazine news pages where the smaller type size required, about eight point, suits the short stories on that page.

Once the grid is chosen, a further decision has to be taken to determine whether the design will be symmetrical (centered) or asymmetrical (off-center). The basic difference is the effect created on the reader by the design chosen. A symmetrical design is fairly safe and staid. Text centered on the page is often balanced out by using graphics at the bottom left- and right-hand corners of the page.

An asymmetric design allows more freedom and the creative use of space, which can be as effective as graphics – more so if you only have poor graphics to work with – and a clean, businesslike effect can be created.

Whichever you choose, don't ever mix the two in one publication. It lacks continuity and makes the reader confused.

## Getting it together

You have defined what you want your publication to achieve and have gathered the relevant words and pictures. Now all you have to do is design and print it – but how best to achieve this?

To begin with, you are limited by physical restraints such as the size of the page, printing process, document binding and the type of paper the publication will be printed on. And unless the publication is a one-off or a new launch, you will also be restrained by the four main typographic parameters which have already been established: line measure, type size, typeface, and line spacing.

Before quantity printing takes place, a decision has to be made whether to use laser printer or phototypeset output as camera-ready artwork. A phototypesetter is used on all professional publications because it gives a sharper image, known as "high resolution." For example, the standard laser printer resolution is around 300 dots to the inch. A phototypesetter has a resolution of 1200 dots to the inch or more. The image becomes sharper, and the type blacker with the increase in dots to the inch. All PostScript (the de facto standard for dtp printing) output applications have the capacity to be sent to a high resolution phototypesetter. This is important to designers and is one of the main reasons for hostility to professional desktop publishing.

The paper upon which your publication is printed can have an important effect on the overall "feel" of the product. There are hundreds of different weights and types of paper available to choose from, although the final choice very often comes down to using what your printer has in stock. Paper surfaces range from the coarse, thick sort often used for headed stationery, to the coated, glossy papers which are used in high-fashion magazines. The general rule is that the smoother the paper, the better able it is to accept fine detail from offset printing plates.

Bear this in mind when you are planning the graphics for your publication. For example, it is virtually useless to commission expensive full-color glossy transparencies for reproduction in a newsletter that will be printed on porous paper; but it is essential for a glossy magazine printed by the photogravure method on coated paper. These magazines, which have highly polished surfaces, often catch the light and can be difficult to read. A publication containing halftones and some color work is best printed on a smooth but matte surface which will not reflect the light but gives good reproduction.

Paper weights are measured in pounds. The term refers to the weight of 500 sheets of the paper in 30 x 22 inch size. As a general guide, the photocopying paper in your office weighs between 20 and 24lb. Heavier weights are available but the measurement system varies from supplier to supplier and one manufacturer's 65lb may be another's 80lb. Check with your local printshop.

The way in which your publication is bound does not really have much effect on a good or bad layout, but once again contributes to the overall "feel" of it. For example, if you have to present a document at a board meeting, it will make a better impression if it is bound, with front and back jackets and, say, a plastic spine holding the pages together, rather than merely having its pages stapled together in the top left-hand corner. For larger documents, the type of binding used will depend on what the printer has available, the way it has been printed and how the document is to be used.

One of the most popular forms of binding is saddle stitching. Pairs of pages are printed together on the same sheet and then stitched or wire stapled together through the fold. Up to 32 pages can be stitched in one section and more than 48 pages will be bound in two sections with the cover drawn around it. Bear in mind that only multiples of four pages are available with center-stitched spreads. Saddle stitching is generally acknowledged as a neat and reliable binding solution.

Another method often used is perfect binding. This is where single sheets are clamped tightly together and a thin layer of glue is applied along the spine. Perfect binding is suitable for thick documents such as a telephone directory. In the commercial publishing world, it is considered a measure of a magazine's success when it moves from saddle stitching to perfect binding because it means the magazine is carrying more pages. When done well, this is a smart-looking way to bind your document. Unfortunately, when perfect binding is imperfect, the spine can fall away and the whole document can come apart.

One of the popular myths surrounding desktop publishing is that it will make printers redundant, with some wits propounding that dtp is an acronym for "death to printers." Nothing could be further from the truth. As more people use computerized publishing methods instead of typewriters or word processors, their need for professional printing services increases rather than decreases. Laser printers do not have the capacity to produce long print runs, especially if the work contains graphics, and the binding services supplied by printing firms are still in demand.

Offset printing is one of the most common types of printing process. You can supply the printer with camera-ready artwork produced on your laser printer and this should consist of clean, high definition black and white prints. From these the printer will make photographs, or film. Once this is done you are really past the stage of no return in your publication. Making corrections to film is extremely expensive so you must ensure that camera-ready artwork (CRA) really is just that. A printer then makes plates from the photographic film, and the plates are positioned on the press. Setting the plates to the right positions can take some time, but once the press is in operation, the print run takes only a few hours, depending on the quantity required. The publication is then bound and wrapped if necessary.

Chapter 1

# Letterheads & Identities

First impressions last...

Letterheads and corporate identities are needed by everyone in business.

Corporate identity is the image a company projects to the outside world. Depending on the size of the company its corporate identity can be made up of many elements - including the way it is perceived by its customers, the financial establishment and the press - but one of the ways in which even the smallest companies try to build up the best possible corporate identity is through excellent and sympathetic graphic design. Every typeface and style used should convey something about the kind of work a company does- electronics, manufacturing baby clothes, running a flower shop and so on. The designer aims to project a sharp image and to unify the range of documents produced with a consistent use of type styles.

One of the most important parts of corporate identity is the company logo.

Company logos should be used consistently, with only a variation in size according to the differing demands placed upon them. For example, a logo would not be used in the same size on a business card as it would on headed stationery. Whatever typeface is used for the company logo, it should not clash with the styles chosen for other company publications. An advantage of desktop publishing is that logos can be saved in a system and not only printed on demand, but also cropped to the appropriate size for different documents.

Most companies use professional designers to help them achieve this. They know something is wrong with their corporate identity, but don't exactly know what. The following pages will show you how to achieve the right look through simple desktop publishing techniques, with emphasis on the quite different looks which can be obtained just by using a variety of typestyles.

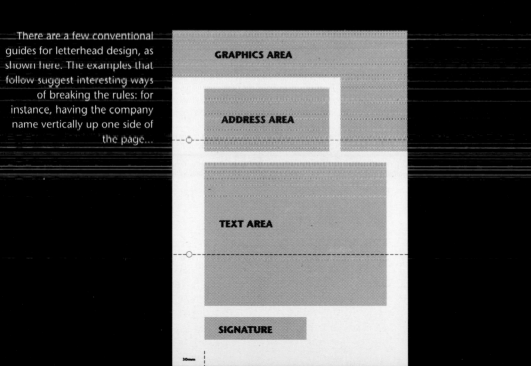

There are a few conventional guides for letterhead design, as shown here. The examples that follow suggest interesting ways of breaking the rules: for instance, having the company name vertically up one side of the page...

GRAPHICS AREA

ADDRESS AREA

TEXT AREA

SIGNATURE

30mm

# ElektroSynth

## (Modern)

Our music equipment company, ElektroSynth, uses the Futura type family and distorted Bodoni to project a modern image. These typefaces are used to good advantage to make short, sharp statements in headlines and captions where their impact is increased through the use of either all uppercase or all lowercase letters. The latter method is used in a company logo which is coupled with an interesting graphic. The graphic is part of a keyboard, thus linking with ElektroSynth's business, but it can also be seen as a capital "E" and so becomes an immediately recognizable symbol for the company.

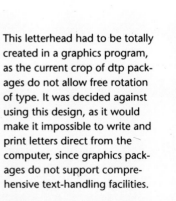

This letterhead had to be totally created in a graphics program, as the current crop of dtp packages do not allow free rotation of type. It was decided against using this design, as it would make it impossible to write and print letters direct from the computer, since graphics packages do not support comprehensive text-handling facilities.

Although this letterhead design was not eventually used, the shape of the triangle coming in from the left hand side was considered a good idea and later used in an ES magazine

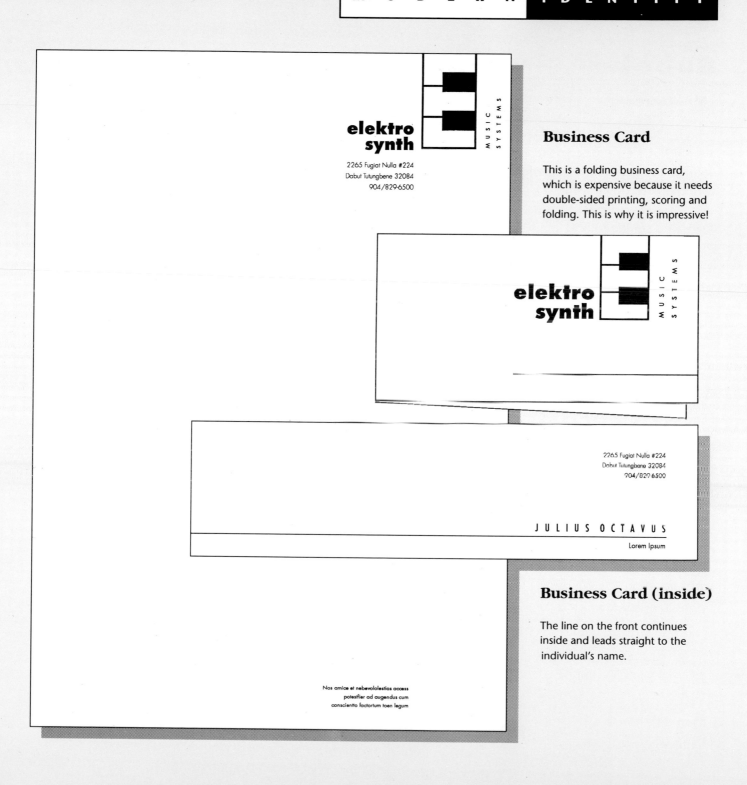

## Business Card

This is a folding business card, which is expensive because it needs double-sided printing, scoring and folding. This is why it is impressive!

## Business Card (inside)

The line on the front continues inside and leads straight to the individual's name.

# Bubbles

## (Mainstream)

Mainstream, or transitional typefaces were chosen for Bubbles, our soap manufacturer. The rounded serifs of Souvenir and Cooper help to soften the letterforms to keep in line with a soft, soapy, bubbly product. This is reinforced by the use of a logo which features a simple bubble graphic and helps the casual observer to quickly assimilate the type of products the company produces.

**Bubbles**

Bubbles Nv.
Klimpostraat 18,
Haag
Nederland N13

*Bubbles*

**Bubbles**

Bubbles Nv.
Klimpostraat 18,
Haag
Nederland N13

*Bubbles*

Nederlands No. 123456
...postraat 18, Haag, Nederland N13

Registered in Nederlands No. 123456
Registered Address: Klimpostraat 18, Haag, Nederland N13

Simple device in the background used to make the letterhead more interesting. A good idea, but in practice it would probably interfere with type if printed in black. It would work well as a custom watermark which would also make forging very difficult.

Note: gray area whited out where address crosses over.

## Cut out

Larger print-runs become more economical when "cutting dies" are used to create interesting effects, like this letterhead with a bubbly top. A simple idea, it would not interfere with written letters.

## Final Letterhead

The horizontal line divides the information and makes it easier to locate the telecommunications information.

## Business Card

The business card is a smaller version of the final lettterhead, with name and job title printed under the logo. The landscape format is more traditional.

## Sticker

Circular cut-out sticker which incorporates the logo's bubble as part of the integral design.

# VAC Chemical

## (Industrial)

VAC Chemical is a no-nonsense industrial manufacturer – a serious business. The typefaces chosen to convey this image are Franklin Gothic Heavy (for headlines) and Century Schoolbook (for body copy). This gives a useful combination of a serif and a sans serif font enabling most design problems to be adequately solved.

End of rule gives an indication of width of margin and provides a point of easy alignment for typewriters, when the address is being typed in.

VAC CHEMIKALIEN AG   LOREM IPSUM 13   D–5800 SUSCIPIT 2
Telefon: (0349) 14 26 97   Fernschreiber: 512291 VAC D   Telefax: (0349) 19 71 23
H.R. 567123 Bonn

Centered layout with address in capital letters.

Simple, balanced layout with full bleed rule following company details.

**VAC Chemikalien AG**
Lorem Ipsum 13        D–5800 Suscipit 2
Telefon: (0349) 14 26 97   Fernschreiber 1 97 123 VACC D

VAC
*Chemikalien*

**VAC Chemikalien**

VAC Chemikalien AG
Lorem Ipsum 13
D–5800 Suscipit 2

Telefon: (0349) 14 26 97
Fernschreiber: 512291 VAC D
Telefax: (0349) 19 71 23

Datum

Ihre Zeichen

Unsere Zeichen

Die Gesellschaft besteht im Namen und zur Rechnung der
VEREINIGTE ALLGEMEINE CHEMIKALIEN AKTIENGESELLSCHAFT VAC CHEMIKALIEN
Suscipit und Deus

Letterhead must contain both
logo and short name,
plus full name.

Address and phone
numbers separated.

Location for date gives vertical
point for type to fit in a window
envelope.
Spaces are increments of
12 point so letterhead can be
typed over with a conventional
typewriter.

The company logo or trademark
is the principal element of the
corporate identity and it should
be used repeatedly and consistently over all official stationery.

**Dipl.Ing. Peter Braun**
Produktionsleiter

**VAC Chemikalien AG**
Lorem Ipsum 13
D–5800 Suscipit 2

Telefon: (0349) 14 26 97
Fernschreiber: 512291 VAC D
Telefax: (0349) 19 71 23

## Business Card

Final letterhead gives legal
details at the bottom of the
page. This contains full name
and phone number, and the
names of directors.

# Bull & Smith

## (Classical)

Classical or old style typefaces, as used by our accountancy firm, project an image of a bygone age and in so doing give the reader a feeling of security, making the firm seem to be old and established and therefore reliable. Baskerville and Caslon were used by Bull & Smith to help them project this image.

**BULL**

**CHARTERED & ACCOUNTANTS**

**SMITH**

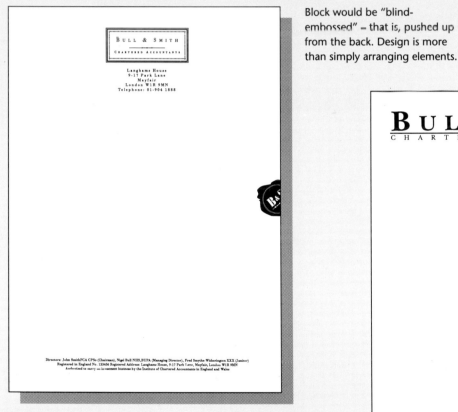

Block would be "blind-embossed" – that is, pushed up from the back. Design is more than simply arranging elements.

Position of type too close to rule. This could only be seen on printout.

Directors' names and legal information centered across the bottom of the page to achieve balance with the top.

Letterspaced capitals give a modern feel to this letterhead whilst retaining the classical "you can trust us" effect given out by the typeface.

Running type around circles is an instant feature of some design programs, which would normally take expensive hours to do manually.

Different effects can be achieved simply by adding text and with the careful use of letterspacing.

This was chosen as a device to accompany the actual type of the logo. Used creatively, side elements like this can strengthen an image.

# Z Mode

### (Contemporary)

Our fashion company needs to project an image which is at the leading edge of graphic design and will reinforce, in the minds of the customers, the idea that the clothes wil be ultra-fashionable too. The use of a simple, yet bold and striking, logo helps to make a direct statement, as do the special symbols contained in the Zapf dingbats type font (for example, the star and the "turn over" arrow) and the repeated use of distorted type.

Putting the name vertically– why not ? It is just as legible, and allows more space for the letter. Most people like to leave a big left-hand margin on business letters.

A design like this would work much better in color, though this is probably not feasible if letters are to be run directly off the laserpinter from blank paper.

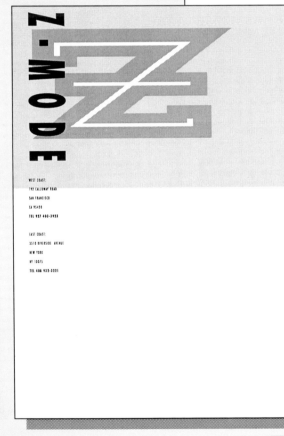

This was chosen as the final logo because it was the most read-able from a distance. Here the whole name has been fitted into one block for use as a tag on jeans pockets.

## Final Letterhead

This position has been chosen
for the logo because it converts
well across the whole identity
and can be used in the same
place on a range of publications
such as the newsletter.

## Business Card

192 CALLOWAY ROAD
SAN FRANCISCO
CA 95420

TEL 408 932-3221

GEORGE LORUM

(PRINCIPAL)

WEST COAST:

192 CALLOWAY ROAD

SAN FRANCISCO

CA 95420

TEL 927 403-3923

EAST COAST:

3510 RIVERSIDE AVENUE

NEW YORK

NY 10075

TEL 408 932-3221

Arrangement and position of
the address in an unusual place
makes the letterhead look
more modern.

Chapter 2

# Sales Material

Desktop wheeler-dealing

Sales material must have a high profile design because its purpose is to be seen and read by customers and the public to induce them to buy goods or services. If customers are put off by a badly designed publication, the company will soon be out of business. The rules for sales material describing products and services are simple: clear, concise editorial combined with an easy-to-read typeface, the inclusion of price information and graphics, where appropriate, which will allow the reader to see what he or she is buying.

At a subliminal level, you are also selling the company. A confused layout badly printed on low grade paper, will automatically lead customers to think of a confused company with low grade products. A smart layout, including a well designed corporate logo, a simple typeface, with words and pictures arranged to best advantage, will give customers an impression of profitability, reliability and stability.

Desktop publishing can help to produce good-looking sales material at relatively cheap cost. Although it may not be possible to produce a full-color glossy catalog or a ten-foot poster directly from your desktop, the typographic foundations can be laid, with four-color artwork dropped in later by your printing firm. However, monochrome work such as classified advertisements, price lists and invitations can all be produced with ease – a morning's work for a proficient desktop publisher. The following pages show you how to create the best visual effect for each particular task.

Before designing your sales material, you should be aware of the strengths and weaknesses of the various formats available:

## Gatefold

Provides six equal-sized panels, but beware of where folds will fall on your type. This format is good for "taster"-style direct mail and promotional material. By opening the fold, the target has confirmed their interest in the product, and will be more willing to look sympathetically at what is inside.

## Concertina Fold

This format has less of an "inside and outside" feel than the gatefold, thus more of the space can be used.

## Shelf Wobbler

There are hundreds of formats for below-the-line sales promotion. Here is an object that would be attached to a supermarket shelf.

# Price Lists

A price list is one of the most precious sales aids, but is one that is most often overlooked. From a design point of view, there may not be much to get excited about. A price list is generally composed of one or two columns of text describing the product, with a price in a separate column. Since the price information is the most important in this document, it should be easy to find. A little thought can turn a dull document into something that the customer will want to keep. The advantage of producing a price list on a desktop publishing system is that it can be kept up-to-date with very little effort and printed in small quantities on a laser printer so that out-of-date stock is not taking up valuable space in a storeroom.

## Offer Prices Sheet

Bubbles' market is well-known for its "below-the-line" promotions, so the graphics would merely state this in the most basic, eye-catching way through the use of direct marketing copy: "Special offer!", "Buy two, get one free!".

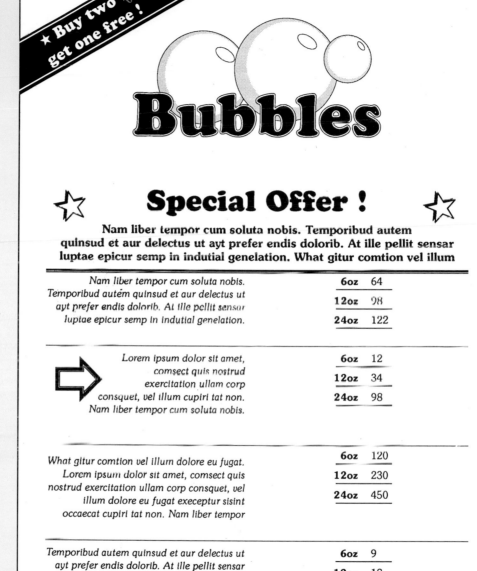

Spaces have been left under the prices so salesmen can negotiate particular deals.

## Basic Price List

Similar style to the company's invoice and statement stationery. Spacious look achieved through the use of a sans serif typeface, leading and letterspaced caps in the heading. House style is maintained in an easy-to-read document.

P R I C E   L I S T

**elektro synth**
MUSIC SYSTEMS

2265 Fugiat Nulla #224
Dabut Tutungbene 32084
904/829-6500

| Nebeval | Access Ipsum | Olestias |
|---------|--------------|----------|
| XR 1234 | Nam liber tempor cum soluta nobis. Temporibud autem quinsud et aur delectus ut ayt prefer en dis dolorib. At ille pellit sensar luptae epicur semp in indutial genelation. What gitur comtion vel illum dolore eu fugat. | 923.00 |
| XR 1235 | Lorem ipsum dolor sit amet, comsect quis nostrud exercitation ullam corp consquet, vel illum dolore eu fugat execeptur sisint occaecat cupiri tat non. | 1134.89 |
| XR 1236 | Lliber tempor cum soluta nobis. Temporibud autem quinsud et aur delectus ut ayt prefer endis dolorib. At ille pellit sensar luptae epicur semp in indutial genelation. | 1546.56 |
| XR 1237 | What gitur comtion vel illum dolore eu fugat. Lorem ipsum dolor sit amet, comsect quis nostrud exercitation ullam corp consquet, vel illum dolore eu fugat execoptur sisint occaecat cupiri tat non. Nam liber tempor cum soluta nobis. | 1465.23 |
| XR 1238 | Temporibud autem quinsud et aur delectus ut ayt prefer endis dolorib. At ille pellit sensar luptae epicur semp in indutial genelation. | 54.50 |

## 3-fold Price List (cover)

Front would be printed in color in huge quantities to take advantage of economies of scale. Spaces would be left in back pages which could be overprinted in cheap black ink as prices fluctuate.

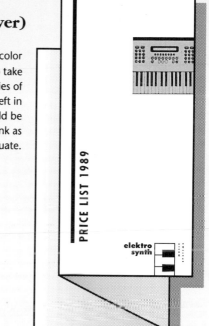

## 3-fold Price List (inside)

Distortion of images lends modernity while still being recognizable. The horizontal compression of PostScript images is created with the resizing facility in the program.

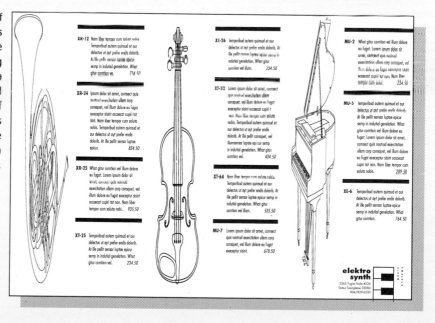

This item is designed around three folds, and images are carefully placed accordingly, so no artwork will fall on the folds.

Monochrome, clear design suited to printing on special paper. An opportunity not available for advertisements.

## Price List Booklet

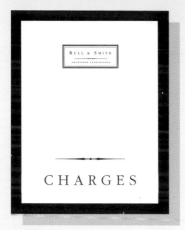

Accountants are usually cautious about having their charges put into print. BUT...

Cover for a small booklet justifying charges. It was decided to put the word "charges" nice and big, in case people thought B&S were being sly about money – not a good image for CPAs!

Thin line and thick/thin rule join to form box.

Page from a price list booklet hence no logo.

Items separated by centered rule.

Text ranged right to the center of the box.

First word in upper case draws the eye.

# BULL & SMITH

## *Charges*

LOREM ipsum dolor sit amet, comsect quis nostrud exercitation ullam corp consquet, vel illum  *£40 per hour*

EXCEPTUR sisint occaecat cupiri tat non. Nam liber tempor cum soluta nobis. Temporibud  *£30 per hour*

AUR delectus ut ayt prefer endis dolorib. At ille pellit sensar luptae epicur semp in indutial  *£15 per hour*

WHAT gitur comtion vel illum dolore eu fugat. Lorem ipsum dolor sit amet, comsect quis  *£60 per hour*

ULLAM corp consquet, vel illum dolore eu fugat execeptur sisint occaecat cupiri tat non  *£75 per hour*

NAM liber tempor cum soluta nobis. Temporibud autem quinsud et aur delectus ut ayt  *£100 per hour*

AT ILLE pellit sensar luptae epicur semp in indutial genelation. What gitur comtion  *£100 per hour*

LOREM ipsum dolor sit amet, comsect quis nostrud exercitation ullam corp consquet  *£45 per hour*

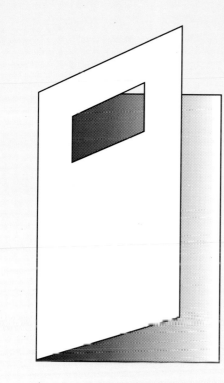

## Folded-sheet Price Card

To make this list more interesting in a classy way, it was decided to use a cover with a cutout where the logo on the inside page would show through.

A one-sheet price list has to have an immediate impact on the reader. Hence short descriptive paragraphs coupled with easy-to-see price information.

"Ph", an abbreviation of per hour, was used as it was felt to be a more tasteful way of presenting charges than "hourly rate."

---

BULL & SMITH
CHARTERED ACCOUNTANTS

### C H A R G E S

*Lorem*
ipsumdolorsit amet, comsect quis
nostrud exercitation ullam corp
consquet, vel illum
**£70ph**

*Execeptur*
sisint occaecat cupiri ut non. Nam
liber tempor cum soluta nobis.
Temporibud
**£120ph**

*Aur*
delectus ut ayr prefer endis dolorib.
At ille pellit sensar luptae epicur semp
in indutial
**£90 ph**

*What*
gitur comtion vel illum dolore eu
fugat. Lorem ipsum dolor sit amet,
comsect quis
**£65ph**

*Ullam*
corp consquet, vel illum dolore eu
fugat execeptur sisint occaecat cupiri
tat non
**£45ph**

## Price List Booklet

Large company logo on cover
for promotion of name.

Main heading formed from
combination of corporate body
text (italicized) and headline
fonts.

State the month price list is
valid, company name and
address.

Sections separated by
a large rule.

Subsections are separated by a
thinner rule, shorter than the
section rule.

The sequence of illustration, part
number, description, is followed
consistently in the same vertical
order to enable people to locate
what they want easily.

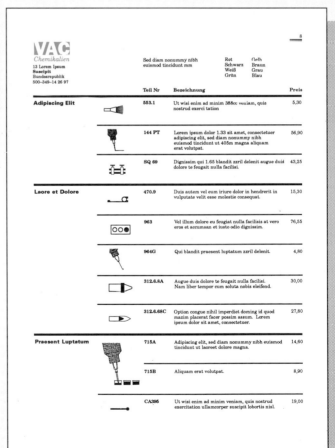

## Inside Page from Price List Book

## One-page Price List

Company logo in prominent position. Graphics can easily be resized for optimum positioning.

Heavy horizontal lines separate product groups.

Light lines aid the eye in reading information across columns.

Gray areas delineate columns.

Company name and address provide contact point when placing order/for more information.

# PREISLISTE

*Chemikalien*

| | Adipiscing Elit | Nibh | Laoreet | Diam |
|---|---|---|---|---|
| **Luptatum Magnum** | | | | |
| | Diam Nonummy Nibh Euismod | 4/22/777 | Diam Nonu | 2-777 |
| | Feugiat Nulla Facilisis At | 1/32/867 | Nibh | 2-867 |
| | Vero Eros Et Accumsan Et | 8/34/866 | Euismod | 4-866 |
| | Iusto Odio Dignissim Qui | 1/32/867 | Laoreet | 2-867 |
| | Blandit Praesent Luptatum | 3/52/862 | Dolore | 2-862 |
| | Zzril Delenit Augue Duis | 4/32/447 | Feugiat | 2-447 |
| | Feugiat Nulla Facilisis At Vero | 9/22/861 | Nulla | 2-861 |
| | Eros Et Accumsan Et Iusto | 3/31/866 | Facilisis | 1-866 |
| | Odio Dignissim Qui Blandit | 4/31/168 | At Vero | 1-168 |
| | Diam Nonummy Nibh Euismod | 1/32/867 | Eros Et | 2-867 |
| | Feugiat Nulla Facilisis At | 6/32/864 | Accumsan | 2-864 |
| | Vero Eros Et Accumsan Et | 8/37/864 | Et Iusto | 7-864 |
| **Lorem Ipsum Dolor** | | | | |
| | Diam Nonummy Nibh Euismod | 7/32/866 | Odio | 2-866 |
| | Feugiat Nulla Facilisis At | 1/32/867 | Dignissim | 2-867 |
| | Vero Eros Et Accumsan Et | 9/42/892 | Qui | 2-892 |
| | Iusto Odio Dignissim Qui | 1/32/867 | Blandit | 2-867 |
| | Blandit Praesent Luptatum | 2/34/965 | Praesent | 4-965 |
| **Feugiat Nulla Ore** | | | | |
| | Meugiat Pulla Gacilisis Lat | 2/37/862 | Luptatum | 7-862 |
| | Vero Eros Et Accumsan Et | 1/32/867 | Zzril | 2-867 |
| | Iusto Odio Dignissim Qui | 7/65/833 | Delenit | 5-833 |
| | Blandit Praesent Luptatum | 6/36/866 | Augue | 6-866 |
| **Aliquam Erat** | | | | |
| | Gusto Odio Dignissim Qui | 2/32/862 | Duis | 2-862 |
| | Blandit Praesent Luptatum | 1/32/867 | Dolore Te | 2-867 |
| | Zzril Delenit Augue Duis | 3/32/863 | Feugait | 2-863 |

**VAC** *Chemikalien*

## Ut Wisi Enim Ad Minim ImpritumVeniam

1212 Quis Nostrud, Exerci Tation, Ullamcorper
Suscipit Lobortis Nisl Ut Aliquip

## Cover

Novel format chosen for this publication. The idea is to attract attention – the shape is as important as the decoration.

Laser printers will allow you to produce finished dummies which can either be used for market research, or just to gain a physical feel for the product.

## Price List (1)

This pictorial version of the list is more suitable perhaps for the kids' lines! However, if diagrams or sketches are available, they're worth thousands of words.

## Price List (2)

This is a self-contained (needs no cover) one-page price list – cheaply and easily printed or photocopied, and economical to distribute.

Name repeated to reinforce the pure graphic of the logo.

Simple horizontal rules unite items and allow the reader to skip across the line to find (a) item and (b) price information immediately.

Prices have a consistent format so comparisons can be made.

The descriptions are set small to allow a lot of information to be given. Text ranged left so it is immediately associated with the product.

The page is divided into the same zones as always to give a consistent look across all documents.

Products are clearly listed in one column. They are ranged right so there is no big gap until the descriptions appear.

Z-MODE CLOTHING ✳

# PRICES

✳ JANUARY 1990

| | | | |
|---|---|---|---|
| **LOREM IPSUM DOLOR** | Lorem ipsum dolor sit amet, comsect quis nostrud exercitation ullam corp consquet, vel illum dolore au fugat. Lorem ipsum dolor sit amet. Nam liber tempor cum soluta nobis. Temporibud autem quinsud et our delectus ut ayt prefer endis delorb. | S M L | $14.99 $15.37 $17.02 |
| **SIT AMET, COMSECT** | At ile pellit sensar luptae epicur semp in indutial genelation. What gitur comtion vel illum dnlore au fugat. Lorem ipsum dolor sit amet, comsect quis nostrud exercitation ullam corp consquet, vel illum dolore au fugat execaptur sisint occaecat cupiri tat non. Nam liber tempar cum soluta nobis. temporibud autem quinsud et our delectus ut ayt prefer endis delorb. | S M L | $12.50 $12.75 $12.98 |
| **QUIS NOSTRUD** | At ile pellit sensar luptae epicur semp in indutial genelation. What gitur comtion vel illum dolore au fugat. Lorem ipsum dolor sit amet, comsect quis nostrud exercitation ullam corp consquet, vel illum dolore au fugat execaptur sisint occaecat cupiri tat non. | S M L | $59 $62 $64 |
| **EXERCITATION ULLAM** | Nam liber tempor cum soluta nobis. Temporibud autem quinsud et our delectus ut ayt prefer endis delorb. At ile pellit sensar luptae epicur semp in indutial genelation. What gitur comtion vel illum dolore au fugat. Lorem ipsum dolor sit amet, comsect quis nostrud exercitation ullam corp consquet, vel illum dolore au fugat execaptur sisint occaecat cupiri tat non. | S M L | $74.23 $80.99 $87.03 |
| **CORP CONSQUET, VEL** | Nam liber tempor cum soluta nobis. Temporibud autem quinsud et our delectus ut ayt prefer endis delorb. At ile pellit sensar luptae epicur semp in indutial genelation. What gitur comtion vel illum dolore au fugat. Lorem ipsum dolor sit amet, comsect quis nostrud exercitation ullam corp consquet, vel illum dolore au fugat execaptur sisint occaecat cupiri tat non. | S M L | $83.50 $84.02 $89.13 |
| **ILLUM DOLORE EU** | Nam liber tempor cum soluta nobis. Temporibud autem quinsud et our delectus ut ayt prefer endis delorb. At ile pellit sensar luptae epicur semp in indutial genelation. What gitur comtion vel illum dolore au fugat. | S M L | $14.99 $15.37 $17.02 |
| **FUGAT EXECEPTUR** | Lorem ipsum dolor sit amet, comsect quis nostrud exercitation ullam corp consquet, vel illum dolore au fugat execaptur sisint occaecat cupiri tat non. Nam liber tempor cum soluta nobis. Temporibud autem quinsud et our delectus ut ayt prefer endis delorb. | S M L | $12.50 $12.75 $12.98 |
| **SISINT OCCAECAT** | At ile pellit sensar luptae epicur semp in indutial genelation. What gitur comtion vel illum dolore au fugat. Lorem ipsum dolor sit amet, comsect quis nostrud exercitation ullam corp consquet, vel illum dolore au fugat execaptur sisint occaecat cupiri tat non. Nam liber tempor cum soluta nobis. Temporibud autem quinsud et our delectus ut ayt prefer endis delorb. | S M L | $14.99 $15.37 $17.02 |
| **CUPIRI TAT NON. NAM** | At ile pellit sensar luptae epicur semp in indutial genelation. What gitur comtion vel illum dolore au fugat. Lorem ipsum dolor sit amet, comsect quis nostrud exercitation ullam corp consquet, vel illum dolore au fugat execaptur sisint occaecat cupiri tat non. Nam liber tempor cum soluta nobis. | S M L | $74.23 $80.99 $82.03 |
| **BULK PURCHASE** | Lorem ipsum dolor sit amet, comsect quis nostrud exercitation ullam corp consquet, vel illum dolore au fugat execaptur sisint occaecat cupiri tat non. Nam liber tempor cum soluta nobis. Temporibud autem quinsud et our delectus ut ayt prefer endis dolorb. | | |

# Catalogs & Brochures

Catalogs come in many shapes and sizes – but usually they are lengthy publications with lots of pictures. Bear in mind that for mail order companies, a catalog generates the primary source of income, so it pays them to invest time and possibly money in an attractive-looking document that people want to buy from. There is a variety of page layouts that can be used in these publications. A catalog page may have many small items and one large item, or a mix of sizes. The overriding consideration is to define a clear style where the reader can obtain all the relevant information about the product from a single page.

## Cover

The use of space gives quality and a "hi-tec" look. The contrast of Bodoni and Futura typefaces adds a human touch to something potentially sterile. The target market is, after all, musicians – not technocrats.

**XZ-234** NOS AMICE ET NEBEVOL OLESTIAS ACCESS QUID

## Inside (1)

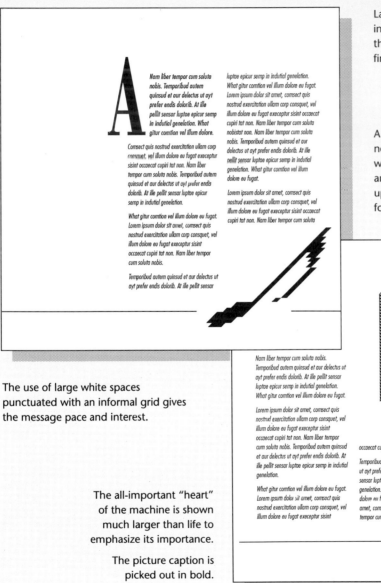

Large indented initial capital in condensed Bodoni leads the eye straight into the bold first paragraph.

A specialist music notation font was distorted and "roughed-up" (bit-mapped) for this graphic.

## Inside (2)

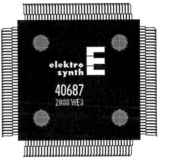

The use of large white spaces punctuated with an informal grid gives the message pace and interest.

The all-important "heart" of the machine is shown much larger than life to emphasize its importance.

The picture caption is picked out in bold.

Inside (4)

## TIP!

Special functions found only in desktop publishing programs can help make the designer's life easier. The "snap to grid" feature, for instance, means that type and graphics will be placed exactly where the designer intends them to go. Measuring by hand or paste-up is no longer needed.

The section heading is set in letterspaced bold capitals.

Using a grid and breaking it allows the columns of text to end at different points.

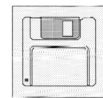

Nebevol olestias access potest lorem.

dolorib. At ille pellit sensar luptae epicur semp in indutial genelation. What gitur comtion vel illum dolore eu fugat.

Nam liber tempor cum soluta nobis. Temporibud autem quinsud et aur delectus ut ayt prefer endis dolorib. At ille pellit sensar luptae epicur semp in indutial genelation. What gitur comtion vel illum dolore eu fugat.

Lorem ipsum dolor sit amet, comsect quis nostrud exercitation ullam corp consquet, vel

illum dolore eu fugat execeptur sisint occaecat cupiri tat non. Nam liber tempor cum soluta nobis. Temporibud autem quinsud et aur delectus ut ayt prefer endis dolorib. At ille pellit sensar luptae epicur semp in indutial genelation.

What gitur comtion vel illum dolore eu fugat. Lorem ipsum dolor sit amet, comsect quis

nostrud exercitation ullam corp consquet, vel illum dolore eu fugat execeptur sisint occaecat cupiri tat non. Nam liber tempor cum soluta

Temporibud autem quinsud et aur delectus ut ayt prefer endis dolorib. At ille pellit sensar luptae epicur semp in indutial genelation. What gitur comtion vel illum.

**NOS AMICE ET NEBEVOL OLESTIAS ACCESS POTEST**

Occaecat cupiri tat non. Nam liber tempor cum soluta Delectus ut ayt prefer endis dolorib. At ille pellit sensar luptae epicur semp in indutial genelation. What gitur comtion vel illum dolore eu fugat.

Nam liber tempor cum soluta nobis. Temporibud autem quinsud et aur delectus ut ayt prefer endis dolorib. At ille pellit sensar luptae epicur semp in indutial genelation. What gitur comtion vel illum dolore eu fugat. Lorem ipsum dolor sit amet, comsect quis nostrud exercitation ullam corp consquet, vel illum dolore eu fugat execeptur sisint occaecat cupiri tat non. Nam liber tempor cum soluta nobis. Temporibud autem quinsud et aur delectus ut ayt prefer endis dolorib. At ille pellit sensar luptae epicur semp in indutial genelation.

What gitur comtion vel illum dolore eu fugat.

Lorem nostri illum occaec cum s

Temporibud autem quinsud et aur delectus ut ayt prefer endis dolorib. At ille pellit sensar luptae epicur semp in indutial genelation. What gitur comtion vel illum dolore eu fugat. Lorem ipsum dolor sit amet, comsect quis nostrud exercitation ullam corp consquet, vel illum dolore eu fugat execeptur sisint occaecat cupiri tat non. Nam liber tempor cum soluta nobis.

Temporibud autem quinsud et aur delectus ut ayt prefer endis dolorib. At ille pellit sensar luptae epicur semp in indutial genelation. What gitur comtion vel illum dolore eu fugat.

Lorem ipsum dolor sit amet, comsect quis nostrud exercitation ullam corp consquet, vel illum dolore eu delectus ut ayt prefer endis

illum dolore eu fugat execeptur sisint occaecat cupiri tat non. Nam liber tempor cum soluta nobis. Temporibud autem quinsud et aur delectus ut ayt prefer endis dolorib. At ille pellit sensar luptae epicur semp in indutial genelation.

What gitur comtion vel illum dolore eu fugat. Lorem ipsum dolor sit amet, comsect quis

nostrud exercitation ullam corp consquet, vel illum dolore eu fugat execeptur sisint occaecat cupiri tat non. Nam liber tempor cum soluta

Temporibud autem quinsud et aur delectus ut ayt prefer endis dolorib. At ille pellit sensar luptae epicur semp in indutial genelation. What gitur comtion vel illum.

Use illustrations that are radically different in size or shape, not all the same size, to give a dynamic look to the layout.

Once again, the picture captions are in bold type.

This graphic was a screen-grab from a specialist sound-editing and sampling program.

Inside (3)

## A new cleanliness you can trust.

*★ Bubbles ★ special offer!*

# Bubbles

## Cover

"Flashes" – the viewer sees more than graphics and reads on...

Diagonals previously produced in a graphics program.

## Double Spread

This is a brochure for a un-willing audience. Consequently the type must be very easy to read. Here a comfortable point size (11) is set on a generous, easy measure (column width). With the friendly typeface (Souvenir), it reads like melting butter.

Flash repeated from cover – check the diagonal margin on the text.

Note external rules on flash – mix/matching old and new styles again.

Subheadings in text attract the eyes of non-willing readers.

Is it a headline or a caption? Cross information – it is below the picture – yet in huge type.

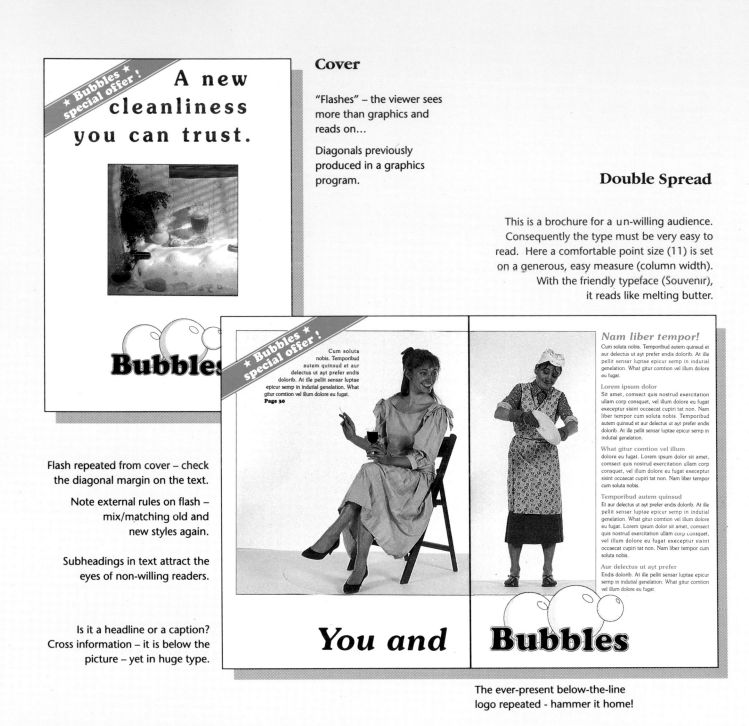

*★ Bubbles ★ special offer!*

Cum soluta nobis. Temporibud autem quinsud et aur delectus ut ayt prefer endis dolorib. At ille pellit sensar luptae epicur semp in indutial genelation. What gitur comtion vel illum dolore eu fugat.
**Page 30**

### Nam liber tempor!

Cum soluta nobis. Temporibud autem quinsud et aur delectus ut ayt prefer endis dolorib. At ille pellit sensar luptae epicur semp in indutial genelation. What gitur comtion vel illum dolore eu fugat.

**Lorem ipsum dolor**

Sit amet, comsect quis nostrud exercitation ullam corp consquet, vel illum dolore eu fugat execeptur sisint occaecat cupiri tat non. Nam liber tempor cum soluta nobis. Temporibud autem quinsud et aur delectus ut ayt prefer endis dolorib. At ille pellit sensar luptae epicur semp in indutial genelation.

**What gitur comtion vel illum**

dolore eu fugat. Lorem ipsum dolor sit amet, comsect quis nostrud exercitation ullam corp consquet, vel illum dolore eu fugat execeptur sisint occaecat cupiri tat non. Nam liber tempor cum soluta nobis.

**Temporibud autem quinsud**

Et aur delectus ut ayt prefer endis dolorib. At ille pellit sensar luptae epicur semp in indutial genelation. What gitur comtion vel illum dolore eu fugat. Lorem ipsum dolor sit amet, comsect quis nostrud exercitation ullam corp consquet, vel illum dolore eu fugat execeptur sisint occaecat cupiri tat non. Nam liber tempor cum soluta nobis.

**Aur delectus ut ayt prefer**

Endis dolorib. At ille pellit sensar luptae epicur semp in indutial genelation. What gitur comtion vel illum dolore eu fugat.

# You and Bubbles

The ever-present below-the-line logo repeated - hammer it home!

## Inside Page (1)

The logo is carefully sized to have the same letter height as the text near it. A large gap is left between the lines to incorporate the Bubbles logo.

Bullet points used for hanging indention.

- Aur delectus ut ayt prefer endis dolorib. At ille pellit sensar luptae epicur semp in indutial genelation.
- Lorem ipsum dolor sit amet, comsect quis nostrud exercitation ullam corp consquet, vel illum dolore eu fugat execeptur sisint occaecat
- What gitur comtion vel illum dolore eu fugat. Lorem ipsum dolor sit amet, comsect quis nostrud exercitation ullam corp consquet, vel illum dolore eu.
- Temporibud autem quinsud et aur delectus ut ayt prefer.

# A clean home, a pampered you - new from Bubbles

**Nam liber tempor** cum soluta nobis. Temporibud autem quinsud et aur delectus ut ayt prefer endis dolorib. At ille pellit sensar luptae epicur semp in indutial genelation. What gitur comtion vel illum dolore eu fugat.

Lorem ipsum dolor sit amet, comsect quis nostrud exercitation ullam corp consquet, vel illum dolore eu fugat execeptur sisint occaecat cupiri tat non. Nam liber tempor cum soluta nobis. Temporibud autem quinsud et aur delectus ut ayt prefer endis dolorib. At ille pellit sensar luptae epicur semp in indutial genelation.

**What gitur comtion** vel illum dolore eu fugat. Lorem ipsum dolor sit amet, comsect quis nostrud exercitation ullam corp consquet, vel illum dolore eu fugat execeptur sisint occaecat cupiri tat non. Nam liber tempor cum soluta nobis.

Temporibud autem quinsud et aur delectus ut ayt prefer endis dolorib. At ille pellit sensar luptae epicur semp in indutial genelation. What gitur comtion vel illum dolore eu fugat. Lorem ipsum dolor sit amet, comsect quis nostrud exercitation ullam corp consquet, vel illum dolore eu fugat execeptur sisint occaecat cupiri tat non. Nam liber tempor cum soluta nobis.

☆ **Temporibud autem quinsud** et aur delectus ut ayt prefer endis dolorib. At ille pellit sensar luptae epicur semp in indutial genelation. What gitur comtion vel illum dolore eu fugat.

**Lorem ipsum dolor** sit amet, comsect quis nostrud exercitation ullam corp consquet, vel illum dolore eu fugat execeptur sisint occaecat cupiri tat non. Nam liber tempor cum soluta nobis. Temporibud autem quinsud et aur delectus ut ayt prefer endis dolorib. At ille pellit sensar luptae epicur semp in indutial genelation. What gitur comtion vel illum dolore eu

**Nam liber tempor** cum soluta nobis. Temporibud autem quinsud et aur delectus ut ayt prefer endis dolorib. At ille pellit sensar luptae

## Inside Page (2)

The star is used as a point of interest and to show where the next important point in the text occurs.

The Illustrations are quick sketches to show where finished photographs would be placed. By outlining such objects on the computer, you can control text runarounds very tightly .

**VAC**
*Chemikalien*

## Gefährliche Werkstoffe

*Vel illum dolore eu feugiat nulla facilisis at vero eros et accumsan et iusto odio dignissim*

## Catalog Cover

Subject of publication in bold type, centered. Thick horizonta lines around the heading emphasize its importance.

## Gefährliche Werkstoffe

**Natriumcyanat**
**NaCNO**

Lorem ipsum dolor sit amet, consectetuer adipiscing elit, sed diam nonummy nibh euismod tincidunt ut laoreet dolore magna aliquam erat volutpat. Ut wisi enim ad minim veniam, quis nostrud exerci tation ullamcorper suscipit lobortis nisl ut aliquip ex ea commodo consequat. Duis autem vel eum iriure dolor in hendrerit in vulputate velit esse molestie consequat, vel illum dolore eu feugiat nulla facilisis at vero eros et accumsan et iusto odio dignissim qui blandit praesent luptatum zzril delenit

augue duis dolore te feugait nulla facilisi. adipiscing elit, sed diam nonummy nibh euismod tincidunt ut laoreet dolore magna aliquam erat volutpat. Ut wisi enim ad minim veniam, quis nostrud exerci tation ullamcorper suscipit lobortis

**Silberthiocyanat**
**AgCNS**

*Lorem ipsum dolor sit amet, c elit, sed diam nonummy nibh e laoreet dolore magna aliquam enim ad minim veniam, quis n lamcorper suscipit lobortis nisl modo consequat. Duis autem hendrerit in vulputate velit ess illum dolore eu feugiat nulla f accumsan et iusto odio dignis luptatum zzril delenit augue d nulla facilisi. adipiscing elit,*

nisl ut aliquip ex ea commodo consequat.
t, sed diam nonummy nibh euismod tincidunt ut laoreet dolore magna aliquam erat volutpat. magna aliquam erat volutpat.
Ut wisi enim ad minim veniam, quis nostrud exerci tation ullamcorper suscipit lobortis nisl ut aliquip ex ea

**VAC**
*Chemikalien*

**2. CYANA**

*Lorem ipsum dolor sit amet, consectetuer ad- ipiscing elit, sed diam*

The page is divided into two columns, with a 5mm gutter. The picture and summary are centered either side of the column, with the summary ranged left.

Section heading reversed out for emphasis.

This logo is used to break up the type's grey effect. Line art, when scanned, can be "traced" from graphics programs.

Ut wisi enim ad minim veniam quis nostrud exerci tation suscipit lobortis nisl ut aliquip ex ea commodo consequat

**Section Cover**

## Pull Out Page

This spread from the brochure is actually designed as a wallchart guide to dangerous substances. The point of brochures is to make your product memorable. If you can provide something useful that makes people keep your brochure, you're halfway there.

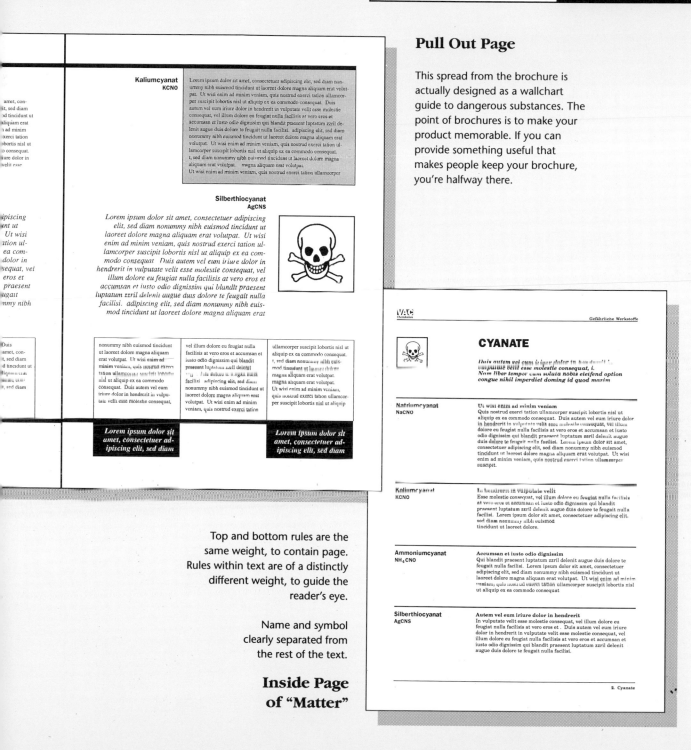

**Kaliumcyanat**
KCNO

Lorem ipsum dolor sit amet, consectetuer adipiscing elit, sed diam nonummy nibh euismod tincidunt ut laoreet dolore magna aliquam erat volutpat. Ut wisi enim ad minim veniam, quis nostrud exerci tation ullamcorper suscipit lobortis nisl ut aliquip ex ea commodo consequat. Duis autem vel eum iriure dolor in hendrerit in vulputate velit esse molestie consequat, vel illum dolore eu feugiat nulla facilisis at vero eros et accumsan et iusto odio dignissim qui blandit praesent luptatum zzril delenit augue duis dolore te feugait nulla facilisi. adipiscing elit, sed diam nonummy nibh euismod tincidunt ut laoreet dolore magna aliquam erat volutpat. Ut wisi enim ad minim veniam, quis nostrud exerci tation ullamcorper suscipit lobortis nisl ut aliquip ex ea commodo consequat. t, sed diam nonummy nibh euismod tincidunt ut laoreet dolore magna aliquam erat volutpat. Ut wisi enim ad minim veniam, quis nostrud exerci tation ullamcorper

**Silberthiocyanat**
AgCNS

Lorem ipsum dolor sit amet, consectetuer adipiscing elit, sed diam nonummy nibh euismod tincidunt ut laoreet dolore magna aliquam erat volutpat. Ut wisi enim ad minim veniam, quis nostrud exerci tation ullamcorper suscipit lobortis nisl ut aliquip ex ea commodo consequat Duis autem vel eum iriure dolor in hendrerit in vulputate velit esse molestie consequat, vel illum dolore eu feugiat nulla facilisis at vero eros et accumsan et iusto odio dignissim qui blandit praesent luptatum zzril delenit augue duis dolore te feugait nulla facilisi. adipiscing elit, sed diam nonummy nibh euismod tincidunt ut laoreet dolore magna aliquam erat

nonummy nibh euismod tincidunt ut laoreet dolore magna aliquam erat volutpat. Ut wisi enim ad minim veniam, quis nostrud exerci tation ullamcorper suscipit lobortis nisl ut aliquip ex ea commodo consequat. Duis autem vel eum iriure dolor in hendrerit in vulputate velit esse molestie consequat,

vel illum dolore eu feugiat nulla facilisis at vero eros et accumsan et iusto odio dignissim qui blandit praesent luptatum zzril delenit augue duis dolore te feugait nulla facilisi adipiscing elit, sed diam nonummy nibh euismod tincidunt ut laoreet dolore magna aliquam erat volutpat. Ut wisi enim ad minim veniam, quis nostrud exerci tation

ullamcorper suscipit lobortis nisl ut aliquip ex ea commodo consequat. t, sed diam nonummy nibh euismod tincidunt ut laoreet dolore magna aliquam erat volutpat. magna aliquam erat volutpat. Ut wisi enim ad minim veniam, quis nostrud exerci tation ullamcorper suscipit lobortis nisl ut aliquip

Lorem ipsum dolor sit amet, consectetuer adipiscing elit, sed diam

Lorem ipsum dolor sit amet, consectetuer adipiscing elit, sed diam

**Gefährliche Werkstoffe**

## CYANATE

Duis autem vel eum iriure dolor in hendrerit in vulputate velit esse molestie consequat, i. Nam liber tempor cum soluta nobis eleifend option congue nihil imperdiet doming id quod maxim

**Natriumcyanat**
NaCNO

Ut wisi enim ad minim veniam
Quis nostrud exerci tation ullamcorper suscipit lobortis nisl ut aliquip ex ea commodo consequat. Duis autem vel eum iriure dolor in hendrerit in vulputate velit esse molestie consequat, vel illum dolore eu feugiat nulla facilisis at vero eros et accumsan et iusto odio dignissim qui blandit praesent luptatum zzril delenit augue duis dolore te feugait nulla facilisi. Lorem ipsum dolor sit amet, consectetuer adipiscing elit, sed diam nonummy nibh euismod tincidunt ut laoreet dolore magna aliquam erat volutpat. Ut wisi enim ad minim veniam, quis nostrud exerci tation ullamcorper suscipit.

**Kaliumcyanat**
KCNO

In hendrerit in vulputate velit
Esse molestie consequat, vel illum dolore eu feugiat nulla facilisis at vero eros et accumsan et iusto odio dignissim qui blandit praesent luptatum zzril delenit augue duis dolore te feugait nulla facilisi. Lorem ipsum dolor sit amet, consectetuer adipiscing elit, sed diam nonummy nibh euismod tincidunt ut laoreet dolore.

**Ammoniumcyanat**
NH$_4$CNO

Accumsan et iusto odio dignissim
Qui blandit praesent luptatum zzril delenit augue duis dolore te feugait nulla facilisi. Lorem ipsum dolor sit amet, consectetuer adipiscing elit, sed diam nonummy nibh euismod tincidunt ut laoreet dolore magna aliquam erat volutpat. Ut wisi enim ad minim veniam, quis nostrud exerci tation ullamcorper suscipit lobortis nisl ut aliquip ex ea commodo consequat

**Silberthiocyanat**
AgCNS

Autem vel eum iriure dolor in hendrerit
In vulputate velit esse molestie consequat, vel illum dolore eu feugiat nulla facilisis at vero eros et. Duis autem vel eum iriure dolor in hendrerit in vulputate velit esse molestie consequat, vel illum dolore eu feugiat nulla facilisis at vero eros et accumsan et iusto odio dignissim qui blandit praesent luptatum zzril delenit augue duis dolore te feugait nulla facilisi.

2. Cyanate

Top and bottom rules are the same weight, to contain page. Rules within text are of a distinctly different weight, to guide the reader's eye.

Name and symbol clearly separated from the rest of the text.

## Inside Page of "Matter"

**BULL & SMITH**
CHARTERED ACCOUNTANTS

*Pension Service*

B&S

## Section Page

Lots of white space gives a comfortable and quiet feeling to the reader.

Section heading in letterspaced caps and small caps.

P E N S I O N   S E R V I C E

*For the young*

Lorem ipsum dolor sit amet, comsect quis nostrud exercitation ullam corp consquet, vel illum dolo1re eu fugat execceptur sisint occaecat cupiri tat non.

Nam liber tempor cum soluta nob1is. Temporibud autem quinsud et aur delectus ut ayt prefer endis dolorib. At ille pellit sensar luptae epicur semp in indutial genelation.

What gitur comtion vel illum dolore eu fugat. Lorem ipsum dolor sit amet, comsect quis nostrud exercitation ullam corp consquet, vel illum dolore eu fugat execceptur sisint occaecat cupiri tat non. Nam liber tempor cum soluta nobis. Temporibud autem quinsud et aur delectus ut ayt prefer endis dolorib.

♠*Page five*♠

## Cover

These corners immediately convey the image of an old-fashioned ledger book, with protective leather-bound corners.

Page numbers are written out in full – a nice touch, but this would probably have to be done by hand, as auto-page numbering is usually numerals only and would be complex for large numbers.

## Inside Spread
Two-column grid with large margins to give upmarket feel.

Considered levels of subheading: small caps then bold italics.

MPOR CUM SOLUTA
ud autem quinsud et
t prefer endis dolorib.
ar luptae epicur semp
tion.
ation vel illum dolore

m dolor sit amet,
ostrud exercitation
uet, vel illum dolore
etur sisint occaecat
am liber tempor cum
emporibud autem
electus ut ayt prefer
At ille pellit sensar
semp in indutial

◆

OMTION VEL ILLUM
GAT. Lorem ipsum
omsect quis nostrud
ill com exercitation, vel
ugat execeptur sisint
tat non. Nam liber
a nobis.
utem quinsud et aur
fer endis dolorib.
ensar luptae epicur
gnelation. Whut gitur
m dolore eu fugat.
or sit amet, comsect
rcitation ullam corp

consquet, vel illum dolore eu fugat
execeptur sisint occaecat cupiri tat non.
Nam liber tempor cum soluta nobis.

Temporibud autem quinsud et aur
delectus ut ayt prefer endis dolorib. At
ille pellit sensar luptae epicur semp in
indutial genelation. What gitur comtion
vel illum dolore eu fugat.

LOREM IPSUM DOLOR SIT AMET,
COMSECT QUIS NOSTRUD.
Exeroitation ullam corp consquet, vel
illum dolore eu fugat execeptur sisint
occaecat cupiri tat non. Nam liber
tempor cum soluta nobis.

☞ *Temporibud autem quinsud et aur
delectus ut ayt prefer endis dolorib. At ille
pellit sensar luptae epicur semp in indutial
genelation. What gitur comtion vel illum
dolore eu fugat.*

☞ *Nam liber tempor cum soluta nobis.
Temporibud autem quinsud et aur delectus
ut ayt prefer endis dolorib. At ille pellit
sensar luptae epicur semp in indutial
genelation.*

☞ *What gitur comtion vel illum dolore
eu fugat. Lorem ipsum dolor sit amet,
comsect quis nostrud exercitation ullam
corp consquet, vel illum dolore eu fug.*

☞*Page six*☞

WHAT GITUR COMTION VEL
ILLUM DOLORE EU FUGAT. LOREM
IPSUM DOLOR SIT AMET, COMSECT
QUIS NOSTRUD EXERCITATION
ULLAM CORP CONSQUET, VEL
ILLUM DOLORE EU FUGAT
EXECEPTUR SISINT OCCAECAT
CUPIRI TAT NON. NAM LIBER
TEMPOR CUM SOLUTA NOBIS.

Temporibud autem quinsud et aur
delectus ut ayt prefer endis dolorib. At
ille pellit sensar luptae epicur semp in
indutial genelation. What gitur comtion
vel illum dolore eu fugat. Lorem ipsum
dolor sit amet, comsect quis nostrud
exercitation ullam corp consquet, vel
illum dolore eu fugat execeptur sisint
occaecat cupiri tat non. Nam liber
tempor cum soluta nobis.

✦✦✦✦✦

*Tumporibud autem quinsud et
aur delectus ut ayt prefer endis
dolorib?*
At ille pellit sensar luptae epicur semp
in indutial genelation. What gitur
comtion vel illum dolore eu fugat.

Lorem ipsum dolor sit amet,
comsect quis nostrud exercitation
ullam corp consquet, vel illum dolore
eu fugat execeptur sisint occaecat
cupiri tat non.

Nam liber tempor cum soluta nobis.

Temporibud autem quinsud et aur
delectus ut ayt prefer endis dolorib. At
ille pellit sensar luptae epicur semp in
indutial genelation. What gitur comtion
vel illum dolore eu fugat.

Nam liber tempor cum soluta nobis.
Temporibud autem quinsud et aur
delectus ut ayt prefer endis dolorib.

At ille pellit sensar luptae epicur
semp in indutial genelation.

✦✦✦✦✦

*What gitur comtion vel illum
dolore eu fugat?*
Lorem ipsum dolor sit amet, comsect
quis nostrud exercitation ullam corp
consquet, vel illum dolore eu fugat
execeptur sisint occaecat cupiri tat non.
Nam liber tempor cum soluta nobis.
Temporibud autem quinsud et aur
delectus ut ayt prefer endis dolorib. At
ille pellit sensar luptae epicur semp in
indutial genelation. What gitur comtion
vel illum dolore eu fugat.

Lorem ipsum dolor sit amet,
comsect quis nostrud exercitation
ullam corp consquet, vel illum dolore
eu fugat execeptur sisint occaecat
cupiri tat non. Nam liber tempor cum
soluta nobis.

Temporibud autem quinsud et aur
delectus ut ayt prefer endis dolorib, at
ille pellit sensar luptae epicur semp.

☞*Page seven*☞

Elegant run of Zapf dingbats to separate paragraphs.

Crosshead is centered, in keeping with the rest of the symmetric design.

☞ "Fist" symbols point to hard pieces of information. A simple Zapf dingbat, used to break up grey value of page.

Note how the diamond in the center of the rule neatly breaks two columns.

Smooth curve on type created in LetraStudio – a unique program for doing things like this! But beware of dtp clichés – how we all tired of bitmap type.

This page would only work as an opening page in the brochure, before you get down to the serious business of selling.

## CLOTHING

What gitur comtion vel illum dolore eu fugat. Lorem ipsum dolor sit amet, comsect quis nostrud exercition ullam corp consquet, vel illum dolore eu fugat execeptur sisint occaecat cupiri tat non. Nam liber tempor cum soluta nobis.

Temporibud autem quinsud et aur delectus ut ayt prefer endis dolorib. At ille pellit sensar luptae epicur semp in indutial genelation. What gitur comtion vel illum dolore eu fugat. Lorem ipsum dolor sit amet, comsect quis nostrud exerci-tation ullam corp consquet, vel illum dolore eu fugat execeptur sisint occaecat cupiri tat non. Nam liber tempor cum soluta nobis.

Temporibud autem quinsud et aur delectus ut ayt prefer endis dolorib. At ille pellit sensar luptae epi-cur semp in indutial genelation. What gitur comtion vel illum dolore eu fugat.

Lorem ipsum dolor sit amet, comsect quis nostrud exercition ullam corp consquet, vel illum dolore eu fugat execeptur sisint occaecat cupiri tat non. Nam liber tempor cum soluta nobis. Temporibud autem quinsud et aur delectus ut ayt prefer endis dolorib.

Nam liber tempor cum soluta nobis. Temporibud autem quinsud et aur delectus ut ayt prefer endis dolorib. At ille pellit sensar luptae epicur semp in indutial genelation. What gitur comtion vel illum dolore eu fugat.

Lorem ipsum dolor sit amet, comsect quis nostrud exercitation ullam corp consquet, vel illum dolore eu fugat execeptur sisint occaecat cupiri tat non. Nam liber tempor cum soluta nobis. Temporibud autem quinsud et aur delectus ut ayt prefer endis dolorib. At ille pellit sensar luptae epicur semp in indutial genelation.

To align the baseline type in these two columns, a space in the first column had to be enlarged one point size , to move it down.

## Cover

Drawn graphics can quickly be manipulated – resized, inverted, or line widths changed, for example.

Rotated text. This is impossible to achieve in current page makeup programs which is why a graphics package was chosen to create this piece of artwork.

## Inside

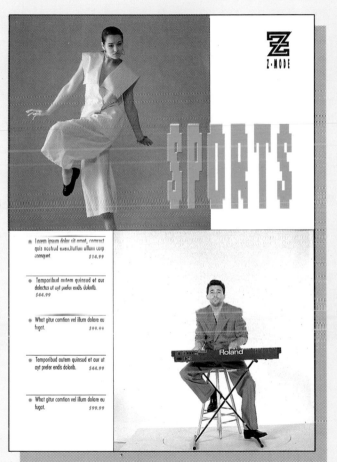

The "Z" logo is repeated in the catalog for instant brand recognition.

The bitmap image gives a "trendy" feel. Remember to take PostScript printer font from your system folder or directory and turn off "bitmap smoothing." The aim is to divide the catalog into sections so that readers can find the information.

Star points say "new object." These would ideally be numbered and cross-linked to objects in the photograph.

Prices are picked out in bold for quick location.

Rules locate descriptions to relevant prices and avoid confusion.

# Presentations

A presentation is one of the most powerful sales aids. Not only do companies have the chance to show their products, but they can also interact with potential clients. Presentations need to create an impact so that people remember the products and services. They can be made using flip charts, overhead foil projectors, 35mm slides, or even on your computer screen. Whichever medium is chosen, the typefaces used should be simple and clean so that they work particularly well in large sizes and can be easily read. The use of simple graphs and charts can help to get the message across even better than words or figures.

This is just an extremely simple presentation from Z-Mode. The company's style is continued, using a dark area at top left. This style is set for the whole presentation, so viewers know where to look for the particular piece of information that they need.

## '95 Objectives

- Lorem ipsum dolor sit amet consectur.
- Nam liber tempor cum soluta nobis temporibud
- Autem quinsud et aur delectus ut
- Epicur semp in indutial lation comtion vel dolore eu fugat.

Always include the company logo for external presentations.

If artwork has been created on an 8 x 11 inch page, always use more than 18 point type. Sans serif is preferable because serifs tend to disappear and blur on projection.

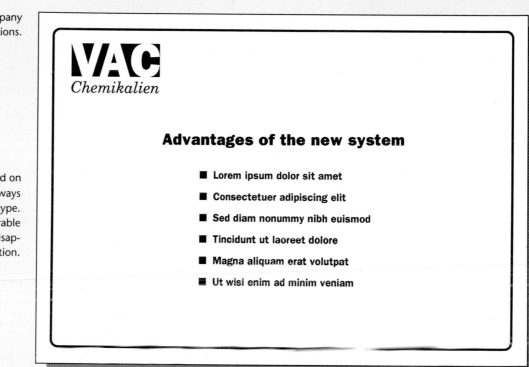

The page setup was "landscape" or "horizontal" to model the proportion of the slide.

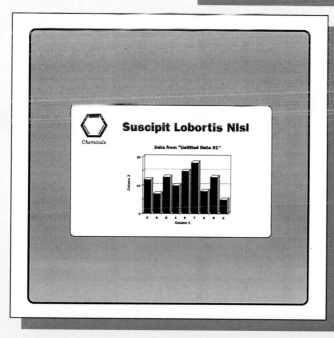

Try to make one point per slide and show another slide for a different point.

## Presentation (1)

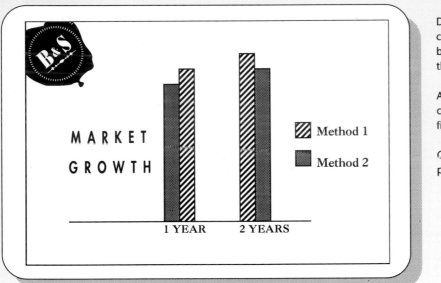

Different types of fill have been chosen that will also work in black and white for a handout of the same work.

A simple visual is an easy way to convey facts which involve figures.

Company logo identifies the presenter.

## Presentation (2)

Use an image appropriate to the business to make the presentation more visually interesting.

Slides should be very simple. Make just one point per slide, not two or twenty-two!

Figures were calculated on a spreadsheet program, then imported into a graphics program to make more impact.

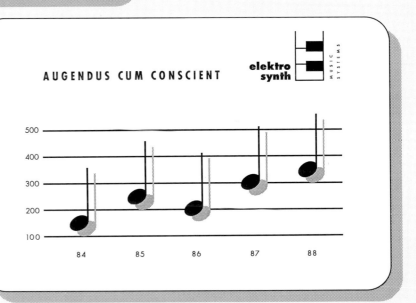

## Presentation (3)

This design would be presented as a running slide show, where the slides would be fading into each other as the speech progressed: almost like an animated film. This keeps the audience's attention.

A simple icon is used to visually indicate important figures.

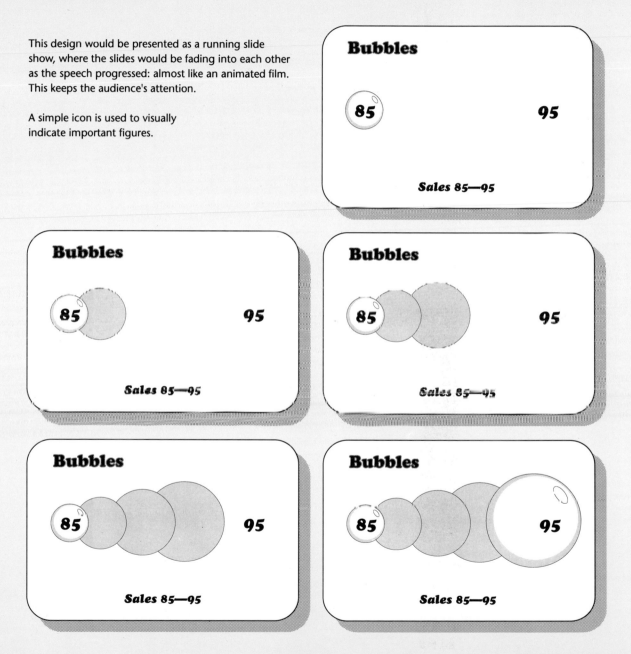

# Advertisements

Promotions and advertisements are intended directly to generate income for a business. There are few rules for designing effective advertisements, but most vital of all is to establish what market the ad is aimed at, the audience it will reach and, finally the medium in which it is to appear - glossy magazine, newsletter, poster and so on. The design of a poster is fundamentally different from, say the design of a magazine advertisement. The large poster needs to use striking visuals with very little text. A magazine ad also needs striking visuals but, as it will be seen close up, it does not need to be so bold, and it will probably contain more text.

This ad imitates the youth-targeted style of design which uses photocopiers to manipulate type. If you move your original as you are photocopying it you get a real flow from the type: an effect widely used by youth magazines. With LetraStudio, a desktop type manipulation package, such ideas take on a whole new perspective.

The "Z" logo and the curved word "Superfashion" were both done in different programs, then brought together in a page make-up system which had the capability to read both file types. Neither graphics program could incorporate the other's work.

## Display Advertisement

Unsubtle display advertisement using very strong "Z" branding. Original graphics, like "Z" logo and starburst, are created in a different program and saved in a compatible format so they can be called up and placed as often as needed.

In desktop publishing, you can try out different sizes and positions of type and graphics until you are satisfied with the result.

EAST COAST:

3510 RIVERSIDE AVENUE

NEW YORK

NY 10075

TEL 408 932-3221

**Z-MODE CLOTHING**

WEST COAST:

192 CALLOWAY ROAD

SAN FRANCISCO

CALIFORNIA

CA 95420

TEL 927 403-3923

DISTRIBUTORS:

WEST COAS:

192 CALLOWAY ROAD

SAN FRANCISCO

CALIFORNIA

CA 95420

TEL 927 403-3923

EAST COAST:

3510 RIVERSIDE AVENUE

NEW YORK

NY 10075

TEL 408 932-3221

**Z-MODE SHOUT!**

## Press Advertisement

Addresses can be fairly small as press ads are seen close-up.

Neat little logo, designed so that it can easily be reproduced on all items of clothing where it can be used as a tag.

The big word to draw in the customers. With desktop publishing there is no distinction between "headline" and "body text" typesetting. It is just as easy to output type in a smaller or bigger size.

## Poster

Arty, attention-getting advert.
It can be used as a poster,
printed one color (not black). This is
an extremely cheap and effective way
of attracting a lot of attention.

## Consumer Advertisement

Small capital letters for authority, italics for spontaneity.

Asymmetrical design will attract attention.

## SIMPLE

## PENSION

## ADVICE

## *now!*

Norem ipsum dolor sit amet, comsect quis nostrud exercitatinn ullam corp consquet, vel illum dolore eu fugat execeptur sisint occaecat cupiri tat non. Nam liber tempor cum soluta nobis. Temporibud autem quinsud et aur delectus ut ayt prefer endis dolorib. Amet, comsect quis nostrud exercitation ullam corp consquet, vel illum dolore eu fugat execeptur sisint occaecat cupiri.

BULL & SMITH
CHARTERED ACCOUNTANTS

## Trade Advertisement

An advertisement which appears in a trade magazine is wordy, going into details of what the company really has to offer.

Big change in font size within the headline creates dynamism.

Use of drop capital creates a more "bookish," "read-me" feel-something the viewer will associate with voluntary reading rather than an advertisement.

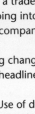

U

illum
occa
por
aute
pref
lupt
tion
dolo
ame
ulla
fuga
non
nob
aur
At i
in i
tion
ipsu
trud
vel
sisir
tem
aute

SIMPLE
PENSION
ADVICE
*now!*

Lorem ipsum dolor sit amet, comsect quis nostrud exercitation ullam corp consquet, vel illum dolore eu fugat execeptur sisint occaecat cupiri tat non. Nam liber tempor cum soluta nobis. Temporibud autem quinsud et aur delectus ut ayt prefer endis dolorib. At pellt sensar luptae epicur semp in indutial genelation.Lorem ipsum dolor sit amet, comsect quis nostrud exercitation ullam corp consquet, vel illum dolore eu fugat execeptur sisint occaecat cupiri.

BULL & SMITH
CHARTERED ACCOUNTANTS

## Poster

Posters have to be "read" very quickly. Therefore, the headline was boxed in a similar style to the logo, so that even if the ad is not read, company awareness is reinforced.

Diagonal margin is achieved by running type around invisible rules. This format leads the eye to the company logo.

*When the going gets tough, The Tough ...*

# TALK TO BULL & SMITH

ipsum dolor sit amet, ct quis nostrud exercita- llam corp consquet, vel u fugat execeptur sisint tat non. Nam liber tem- ta nobis. Temporibud d et aur delectus ut ayt lorib. At ille pellit sensar emp in indutial gencla- tur comtion vel illum t. Lorem ipsum dolor sit quis nostrud exercitation squet, vel illum dolore cu sisint occaecat cupiri tat er tempor cum soluta ibud autem quinsud et ayt prefer endis dolorib. nsar luptae epicur semp elation. What gitur com- dolore eu fugat. Lorem amet, comsect quis nos- n ullam corp consquet, re eu fugat execeptur cupiri tat non. Nam liber luta nobis. Temporibud d et aur delectus ut ayt

prefer endis dolorib. At ille pellit sensar luptae epicur semp in indutial genela- tion. What gitur comtion vel illum dolore eu fugat. Lorem ipsum dolor sit amet, comsect quis nostrud exercitation ullam corp consquet, vel illum dolore eu fugat execep- tur sisint occaecat cupiri tat non. Nam liber tempor cum soluta nobis. Temporibud autem quinsud et aur delectus ut ayt prefer endis dolorib. At ille pellit sensar luptae epicur semp in indutial genelation. What gitur comtion vel illum dolore eu fugat. Lorem ipsum dolor sit amet, com- sect quis nostrud exercitation ullam corp consquet, vel illum dolore eu fugat.Temporibud autem quinsud et aur delectus ut ayt prefer endis dolorib. At ille pellit sensar luptae epicur semp in indutial genelation.

Talk to them first by telephoning 904-1888 Or write to :

Langhams House 9-17 Park Lane Mayfair, London WIR 9MN

## Trade Advertisement

Photo commissioned to bleed into white, from top down.

Large, bold headline acts as lead-in from photograph and delineates photo.

No indention on first paragraph of each new block.

Subheads break up body copy. Increased leading of body text for legibility.

Coupon to be filled in for further information, with company logo and address prominent. Care needs to be taken to ensure coupon is large enough to be filled in, yet not so large that it dominates the ad. Include initials and date of publication as a reference for replies.

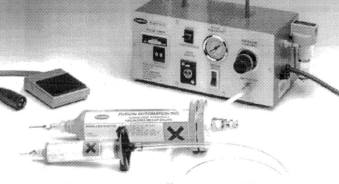

# Dosiergerät von VAC

**Sectetuer adipiscing elit, sed diam nonummy**

Euismod tincidunt ut laoreet dolore magna aliquam erat volutpat. Ut wisi enim ad minim veniam, quis nostrud exerci tation ullamcorper suscipit lobortis nisl ut aliquip ex ea commodo consequat.

Duis autem vel eum iriure dolor in hendrerit in vulputate velit esse molestie consequat, vel illum dolore eu feugiat nulla facilisis at.

**Augue duis**

Vero eros et accumsan et iusto odio dignissim qui blandit praesent luptatum zzril delenit augue duis dolore te feugait nulla facilisi.

Lorem ipsum dolor sit amet, consectetuer adipiscing elit, sed diam nonummy nibh euismod tincidunt est ut laoreet.Dolore magna aliquam erat volutpat. Ut wisi enim ad minim.

Veniam, quis nostrud exerci tation ullamcorper suscipit lobortis nisl ut aliquip ex ea commodo consequat. Duis autem vel eum iriure dolor in hendrerit in vulputate velit esse molestie consequat, vel illum dolore eu feugiat nulla.

**Et iustio odio**

Facilisis at vero eros et accumsan et iusto odio dignissim qui blandit praesent. Luptatum zzril delenit augue duis dolore te feugait nulla facilisiluptatum zzril delenit augue duis dolore te feugait nulla facilisi. Lorem ipsum dolor sit amet, velit esse molestie consequat.

Nobis eleifend option congue nihil:
Imperdiet doming id ☐ quod mazim ☐
Placer ............................... Possim ..................
Facer ................
Anschrift ..........................................

.................................................. Tel. ...................
Sed diam nonummy nibh: VAC Chemikalien
VAC Lorem Ipsum 13
Chemikalien 5800 Suscipit 2 IP15/11

## Response Coupon

Boxes to be ticked are graphics from Zapf Dingbats. Notice how area inside box is white, because font defines an area and then fills it with white. It is better to use a graphic character rather than drawn boxes because the character will flow with the text if any text is changed. Also, it will always have the same x-height as the preceding type.

✄
Nobis eleifend option congue nihil:
**Imperdiet doming id** ☐ **quod mazim** ☐
Placer ..................................... Possim ..................
Facer ..................................................
Anschrift ..........................................
.................................................
.......................................... Tel. ..................
*Sed diam mmy nibh:* VAC Chemikalien
VAC Lorem Ipsum 13
Chemikalien 5800 Suscipit 2 IP15/11

# KEMIKALIEN

## Lorem ipsum $75.000

Lorem ipsum dolor sit amet, consectetuer adipiscing elit, sed diam nonummy nibh euismod tincidunt ut laoreet dolore magna aliquam erat volutpat. Ut wisi enim ad minim suscipit lobortis nisl ut aliquip ex ea commodo consequat. Duis vulputate velit esse molestie consequat, vel illum autem vel eum iriure dolor in hendrerit in vulputate velit esse molestie consequat, vel illum dolore eu feugiat nulla facilisis at vero eros et accumsan et iusto odio dignissim qui blandit praesent luptatum zzril delenit augue duis dolore te feugait facilisi. Dolor sit amet, magna aliquam erat volutpat.

Duis autem vel eum iriure dolor in hendrerit in vulputate velit esse molestie consequat, Lorem vulputate velit esse molestie consequat, vel illum ipsum dolor sit amet, consectetuer adipiscing elit, sed diam nonummy nibh euismod tincidunt ut laoreet dolore magna aliquam erat volutpat. Ut wisi enim ad minim veniam, quis nostrud exerci vulputate velit esse molestie consequat, vel illum tation ullamcorper suscipit wisi enim wisi enim zzril welenit aedril delenitlobortis.

**VAC**
*Chemikalien*

Duis autem vel eum iriure:
Dolor in hendrerit in vulputate velit esse vulput molestie consequat, vel illum dolore eu feugiat nulla facilisis.

## Recruitment Advertisement

This recruitment advertisement uses the corporate typeface (Century).

Capitals for group headlines.

Tinted rules are produced directly from the desktop – no printer strip-in costs.

White space leads the eye to the logo.

## Consumer Advertisement

# Neue PRODUKTE

### DUIS AUTEM VEL EUM IRIURE

Lorem ipsum dolor sit amet, consectetuer adipiscing elit, sed diam nonummy nibh euismod tincidunt ut laoreet dolore magna aliquam erat volutpat.Duis autem vel eum iriure dolor in hendrerit in vulputate velit esse molestie consequat, vel illum dolore eu feugiat nulla facilisis at vero eros et accumsan et iusto odio dignissim qui blandit praesent luptatum zzril delenit augue duis dolore te feugait nulla facilisi. Lorem ipsum dolor sit amet, consectetuer adipiscing elit, sed diam nonummy nibh euismod tincidunt ut laoreet dolore magna aliquam erat volutpat.

### LOREM IPSUM DOLOR SIT

Qui blandit praesent luptatum zzril delenit augue duis dolore te feugait nulla facilisi. Lorem ipsum dolor sit amet, consectetuer adipiscing elit, sed diam nonummy nibh euismod tincidunt ut laoreet dolore magna erat volutpat.Duis autem vel eum iriure dolor in hendrerit in vulputate velit esse molestie consequat, vel illum dolore eu feugiat nulla facilisis at vero eros et delenit augue duis dolore te feugait nulla facilisi. Lorem ipsum dolor sit amet, consectetuer adipiscing elit, sed diam nonummy nibh euismod tincidunt ut laoreet dolore magna aliquam erat volutpa

### UT WISI ENIM AD MINIM

Duis autem vel eum iriure dolor in hendrerit in vulputate velit esse molestie consequat, vel illum dolore eu feugiat nulla facilisis at vero eros et accumsan et iusto odio dignissim qui blandit praesent luptatum zzril delenit augue duis dolore te feugait nulla facilisi. Lorem ipsum dolor sit amet, consectetuer adipiscing elit, sed diam nonummy nibh euismod tincidunt ut laoreet dolore magna aliquam erat volutpat.Duis autem vel eum iriure dolor in hendrerit in vulputate velit esse molestie consequat.

### FISION POSTE SYSTENSUM

Lorem ipsum dolor sit amet, consectetuer adipiscing elit, sed diam nonummy nibh euismod tincidunt ut laoreet dolore magna aliquam erat volutpat. Ut wisi enim ad minim veniam, quis nostrud exerci tation ullamcorper suscipit lobortis nisl ut aliquip ex ea commodo consequat. Duis autem vel eum iriure dolor in hendrerit in vulputate velit esse molestie consequat, vel illum dolore eu feugiat nulla facilisis at vero eros et accumsan et iusto odio dignissim qui bland.

**VAC**
*Chemikalien*  **Lorem Ipsum Aolor Amet**
13 Lorum Ipsum, 5800 Suscipitum 2, Duis Autem At Vero, Tel. 349 14 26 97

## Display Advertisement

Advertisement grid and house style have been created and used to link the ads into an overall campaign.

Specialist typefaces can be used as illustrative designs. Here a music notation font forms the basis of the graphic.

Be careful to ensure that spaces above and below the graphic are equal.

*Temporibud access autem.*

### READ HOW YOUR MUSIC CAN SOUND

Nam liber tempor cum soluta nobis. Temporibud autem quinsud et aur delectus ut ayt prefer endis dolorib. At ille pellit sensar luptae epicur semp in indutial genelation. Whut gitur comtion vel illum dolore eu fugat. Temporibud autem quinsud. Nam liber tempor cum soluta nobis. Temporibud autem.

Lorem ipsum dolor sit amet, comsect quis nostrud exercitation ullam corp consquet, vel illum dolore eu fugat execeptur sisint occ oecat cupiri tat non. Nam liber tempor cum soluta nobis. Temporibud autem quinsud et aur delectus ut ayt prefer endis dolorib. At ille pellit sensar luptae epicur semp in ind utial genelation.

What gitur comtion vel illum dolore eu fugat. Lorem ipsum dolor sit amet, comsect quis nostrud exercitation ullam corp consquet, vel illum dolore eu fugat execeptur sisint occaecat cupiri tat non.

Temporibud autem quinsud et aur delectus ut ayt prefer endis dolorib. At ille pellit sensar luptae epicur semp in indutial genelation. What gitur comtion vel illum dolore eu fugat. Lorem ipsum dolor sit amet, comsect quis nostrud exercitation ullam corp consquet, vel illum dolore eu fugat execeptur sisint occaecat cupiri tat non. Nam liber tempor cum soluta nobis.

Nos amice et nebevol olestias access potest fier ad augendus to factor toen legum.

Oleofios

Access

Potest

**elektro synth**
2265 Fugiat Nulla #224
Dabut Tutungbene 32084
904/829-6500

M U S I C   S Y S T E M S

---

### READ HOW YOUR MUSIC CAN SOUND

Nam liber tempor cum soluta nobis. Temporibud autem quinsud et aur delectus ut ayt prefer endis dolorib. At ille pellit sensar luptae epicur semp in indutial genelation. What gitur comtion vel illum eu fugat.

Lorem ipsum dolor sit amet, comsect quis nostrud exercitation ullam corp consquet, vel illum dolore eu fugat execeptur sisint occaecat cupiri tat non. Nam liber tempor cum soluta.

Temporibud autem quinsud et aur delectus ut ayt prefer endis dolorib. At ille pellit sensar luptae epicur semp in indutial genelation.

What gitur comtion vel illum dolore eu fugat. Lorem ipsum dolor sit amet, comsect quis nostrud exercitation ullam corp consquet, vel illum dolore eu fugat execeptur sisint occaecat cupiri tat non. Nam liber tempor cum soluta nobis.

**elektro synth**
2265 Fugiat Nulla #224
Dabut Tutungbene 32084
904/829-6500

M U S I C   S Y S T E M S

Logo-graphic can be easily imported and resized. This is quicker than using a conventional photo-mechanical transfer.

## Coupon Response Advertisement

Use proper rules, not underlining, for dashed lines to raise the text from the line.

Ensure there is enough space for the coupon to be filled out legibly.

## Poster

## Newspaper Advertisement

In a busy recruitment section of a newspaper, an advertisement needs space and an eye-catching element to attract attention. The bold dotted lines focus the eye on the headline in between.

With effects like these a low-quality original can be "covered up" and made into an interesting image. This is achieved through scanner software which enables the halftone to be reproduced in high contrast, posterized, negative and coarse line-screen versions.

The headline font (Bodoni condensed) is consistent throughout this advertising campaign.

## Poster (1)

This billboard poster is an instantly absorbed, simple idea which works well for an audience with little time to spare.

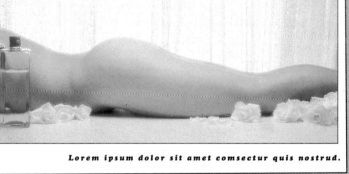

*Bubbles* **is best for Baby's bottom**

*Lorem ipsum dolor sit amet comsectur quis nostrud.*

## Poster (2)

A quick idea to represent a simple slogan. Dtp is not the ideal method for producing finished artwork for billboard poster campaigns, but it will allow you to quickly visualize ideas.

# SALESMEN to 20K

- Nam liber tempor cum soluta nobis. Temporibud
- Autem quinsud et aur delectus ut ayt prefer endis dolorib.
- At ille pellit sensar luptae epicur semp in indutial genelation.
- What gitur comtion vel illum dolore eu fugat.
- Lorem ipsum dolor sit amet, comsect quis nostrud exercitation ullam corp consquet, vel illum

**Bubbles**

**Contact: N Hoogstraten**

**Bubbles Nv., Klimpostraat 18, Haag Nederland N13**
Tel (24) 193 4371 Fax (24) 921 1219

## Recruitment Advertisement

Keep it simple. Information should include job description, salary details and address for response.

Making the copy fit is an easy and instant operation with desktop publishing. For example, stretching the word "salesmen" to the width of the box was achieved instantaneously, whilst maintaining the same letter height.

## Consumer Advertisement

Understated design catches the eye through its simplicity and the use of a striking graphic.  Leader dots after the headline draw the reader to the message.

Explanatory text is deliberately positioned almost as an afterthought. But the type is large enough not to be overlooked.

Inclusion of the logo reinforces the company name.

Flash on the corner identifies the promotion campaign of which this advertisement is part. It may be useful to show new packaging for the campaign period.

Bullet points are used to highlight hard information – items the trade simply must know.

## Trade Advertisement

The white out of black (WOB) block clearly states the proposition to a cynical trade reader.

Coupon response helps the company to correctly target follow-up calls and literature.

# Invitations

The choice of typeface, style, paper, color and even whether or not to use graphics, can say a lot about the event to which you are inviting people. A heavy card with fancy embossed lettering printed in silver or gold gives a completely different message to the typewritten "tear off strip and fill in the blanks" kind of invitation. The aim of a business or marketing invitation is to make the guests feel it will be worth their while to come along and learn about the new products, services and so on – the only means the designer has of communicating all that is good design.

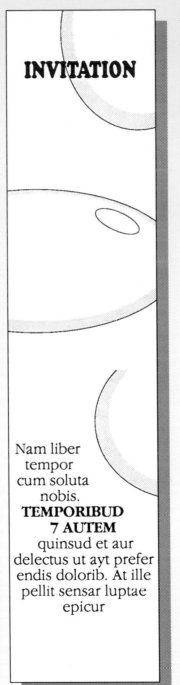

## Mainstream

This strangely shaped invitation is conceived to fit inside a capsule, such as those used in certain medical preparations. Printed on plastic, it floats to the surface when the capsule is dissolved in water. This ties in with Bubbles washing powder which also needs water to dissolve.

These distorted graphics are easily created with "modify graphic" commands.

---

### TIP!

The material upon which the document is printed can also have an effect on design. Heavy embossed paper, or even plastic, are alternatives to standard strong coated or uncoated papers.

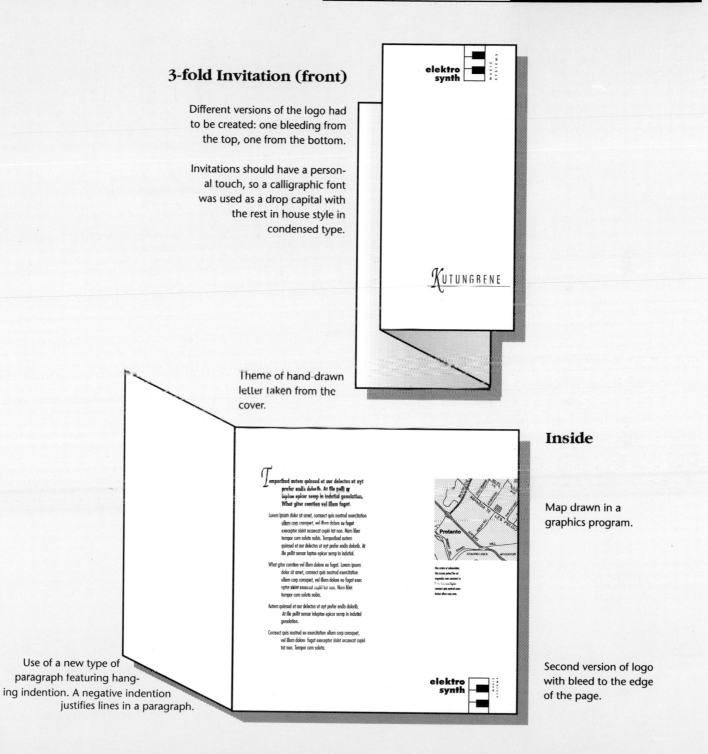

## 3-fold Invitation (front)

Different versions of the logo had to be created: one bleeding from the top, one from the bottom.

Invitations should have a personal touch, so a calligraphic font was used as a drop capital with the rest in house style in condensed type.

**elektro synth**
MUSIC SYSTEMS

𝒦UTUNGRENE

Theme of hand-drawn letter taken from the cover.

## Inside

𝒯*emporibud autem quinsud et aur delectus ut ayt prefer endis doluib. At ille pelli or luptue epicur semp in indutial genelation. What gitur comtion vel illum fugat.*

Lorem ipsum dolor sit amet, comsect quis nostrud exercitation ullam corp roeroyset, vel illum dolore eu fugat execeptur sisint occaecat cupiri tat non. Nam liber tempor cum soluta nobis. Temporibud autem quinsud et aur delectus ut ayt prefer endis dolorib. At ille pellit sensar luptoe epicur semp in indutial.

What gitur comtion vel illum dolore eu fugat. Lorem ipsum dolor sit amet, comsect quis nostrud exercitation ullam corp consquet, vel illum dolore eu fugat exec eptur sisint occaecat cupiri tat non. Nam liber tempor cum soluta nobis.

Autem quinsud et aur delectus ut ayt prefer endis dolorib. At ille pellit sensar inluptoe epicur semp in indutial genelation.

Comsect quis nostrud eu exercitation ullam corp consquet, vel illum dolore fugat execeptur sisint occaecat cupiri tat non. Tempor cum soluta.

Map drawn in a graphics program.

Protanto

**elektro synth**
MUSIC SYSTEMS

Use of a new type of paragraph featuring hanging indention. A negative indention justifies lines in a paragraph.

Second version of logo with bleed to the edge of the page.

Two important features: the company logo
and the word "invitation."

### Outside

Address for
returning reply.

Dotted line shows where the
fold occurs in this invitation.

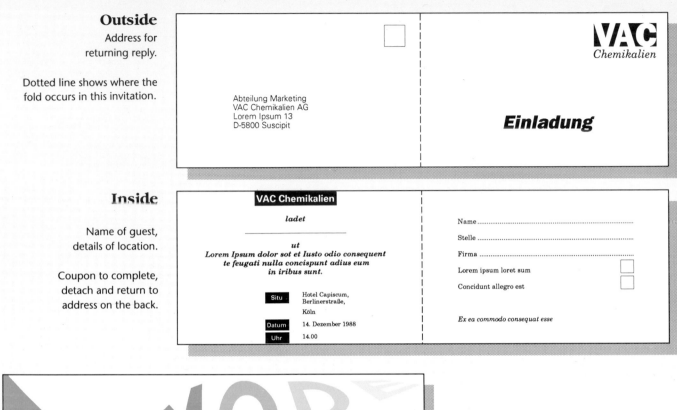

Abteilung Marketing
VAC Chemikalien AG
Lorem Ipsum 13
D-5800 Suscipit

**VAC**
*Chemikalien*

*Einladung*

### Inside

Name of guest,
details of location.

Coupon to complete,
detach and return to
address on the back.

**VAC Chemikalien**

*ladet*

_____

*ut*
*Lorem Ipsum dolor sot et Iusto odio consequent*
*te feugati nulla concispunt adius eum*
*in iribus sunt.*

| Situ | Hotel Capiscum, Berlinerstraße, Köln |
| Datum | 14. Dezember 1988 |
| Uhr | 14.00 |

Name ..............................................................

Stelle .............................................................

Firma .............................................................

Lorem ipsum loret sum

Concidunt allegro est

*Ex ea commodo consequat esse*

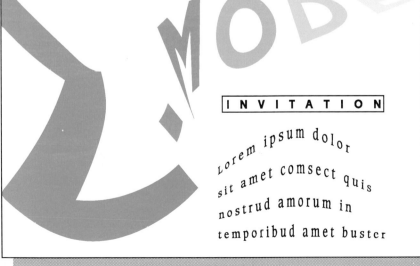

**INVITATION**

*Lorem ipsum dolor sit amet comsect quis nostrud amorum in temporibud amet buster*

Distorted type done on a dtp computer. An effect
like this can be overwhelming and it's easy to get
carried away. Here, the wacky design has been
offset by a clear, simple "invitation" to put the
recipient back in touch with reality.

*Christmas Party*

Bearing in mind the fact
that most Christmas
invitations are for display, or
hanging on strings, a
vertical, self-supporting
format has been chosen.

*Christmas Party*

For a Christmas card, a snowflake
is used as part of the company
logo. Even though the card is for
a fun event, it's still a costly
marketing tool, not to be wasted.

Conventional style to set "at" and
"on" in their own lines.

Simple difference in point sizes
shows up main points.

B&S

BULL & SMITH

*would like to invite*

.................................

*to attend their
1996 Christmas Party
on*
*Friday 19 December 1996*
*at*
*99 Great Portman St
London W1*

*Dress: Formal*

Chapter 3
# Business Forms

Mean it!

The majority of forms and schedules are cheaply produced. Usually they are printed fast, in large quantities, on low-quality paper and the designer needs to bear this in mind when creating the forms. It is also important to think about filing. It may be necessary to leave a margin which will allow holes to be punched into the document. For simplicity, continuity and good design, choose a grid and stick to it for the entire range of business forms.

Desktop publishing can help to achieve consistency in the design of a form and there are various software packages available whose function is specifically to help you design forms on your computer. For example, a lot of legal work involves the use of standard printed forms. Not only do they physically occupy a lot of space, but they are time-consuming to keep track of and expensive to buy. These problems could be overcome by keeping a templet of each form on a desktop publishing system and calling up the relevant item as and when it is needed. The ability to create your own forms, fill them out on screen and print them on a high quality laser device is a revelation to many people.

Desktop publishing really has lifted the art of designing forms. At one time lines and boxes were drawn in pen or with the dash key on a typewriter and the relevant information typed in. Then the whole document was printed on a photocopier or duplicator. If a smart form was required, it had to be sent out to a professional typesetter. Now forms can incorporate your digitized logo, boxes and rules of different weights, and quality typefaces, giving an eye-catching, clean look that people will notice.

## VAC Chemikalien

# Vel Illum Dolore Eu Facilisis

Praesent Luptatum Zzril Delenit Augue  Feugait Nulla
Nonummy Nibh Euismod Tincidunt Ut Laoreet
Tation Ullamcorper Suscipit Lobortis

### Hendrerit Euismod Tincidunt

No. _____

## Nonummy

Duis autem[1] _____

Te Feugait Nulla _____

1  Laoreet dolore magna aliquam erat volutpat. Ut wisi enim ad.

## Laoreet Dolore

Autem Vel[2,3,4] _____

_____

_____

_____

_____

2  Laoreet dolore magna aliquam erat volutpat. Ut wisi enim ad minim.

3  Veniam, quis nostrud exerci tation.

4  Ullamcorper suscipit lobortis nisl ut aliquip ex ea commodo consequat. Duis autem, e.g 23/34/68.

## Wisi Enim

Feugiat Nulla Facilisis[5,6] _____

_____

Velit Esse[7] _____

_____

5  Dolore magna aliquam erat volutpat.UtVeniam, quis nostrud exerci tation wisi enim ad minim.

6  Veniam, quis nostrud exerci tation.

7  Ullamcorper suscipit lobortis nisl ut aliquip ex ea commodo consequat. Duis autem.

## Quis Nostrud Exerci

Molestie Consequat[8,9] _____

_____

Dignissim Qui[10] _____

Delenit Augue Duis Dolore[11] _____

_____

8  Laoreet dolore magna aliquam erat volutpat. Ut wisi enim ad minim.

9  Veniam, quis nostrud exerci tation.

10 Ullamcorper suscipit lobortis nisl ut aliquip ex ea commodo consequat. Duis autem.

11 Veniam, quis nostrud exerci tation.

## Lorem Ipsum Dolor Sit Amet, Consectetuer Adipiscing Elit, Sed Diam

Autem vel eum
Ut Laoreet Dolore

---

The company logo combines with the title of the form and explanatory text.

Gray areas conventionally indicate "for office use only."

Notes set beside boxes to give specific information.

Gray screens interfere with type (especially after printing) so it is essential to send a document such as this one to a high resolution typesetter.

Each box has a name to clarify its purpose.

Final text should tell the reader what to do with the form once it has been filled out.

# Invoices

The design of invoices can, eventually, affect the cash flow of a company, and indeed profitability. A badly designed invoice can, and often does, find its way to the bottom of the pile.

A strong logo is one of the first things to catch the eye and, believe it or not, the word "invoice" should actually appear somewhere on the document so that the recipient is left in no doubt as to what the communication is, and can act on it. Once the important text elements have been assembled, the aim is to produce a simple layout with horizontal and vertical lines of various weights to achieve a neat and tidy look. It may also help to print your invoices on colored paper — that way they will really stand out from the rest of the paperwork in an office.

**MARCEL MARCEAU**
**Pure Group Des Magazins**
47 Rue Des Heroes
Paris 7v

Z-MODE
12 RUE DU FG.
MONTMARTRE
PARIS 9E

| INVOICE NO. | P/1192 |
|---|---|

Details

| | |
|---|---|
| Nam liber tempor cum soluta nobis. Temporibud autem quinsud et aur delectus ut ayt prefer endis dolorib. At ille pellit sensar luptae epicur semp in indutial genelation. What gitur comtion vel illum dolore eu fugat. | 200 |
| Lorem ipsum dolor sit amet comsect quis nustiud exercitation ullam corp consquet | 57 |

| Total Net | 257 |
|---|---|
| VAT à 15% | 38.55 |
| **GRANDE TOTAL** | **295.55** |

Temporibud autem quinsud et aur delectus ut ayt prefer endis dolorib. At ille pellit sensar luptae epicur semp in indutial genelation. What gitur comtion vel illum dolore eu fugat. Lorem ipsum dolor sit amet, comsect quis nostrud exercitation ullam corp consquet, vel illum dolore eu fugat execeptur sisint occaecat cupiri tat non. Nam liber tempor cum soluta nobis.

Strong lines have been drawn on this form so it is equally easy to fill out by hand with spaces being provided. By putting a boxed-in square on the paper you are insisting something is entered, thus minimizing the chance of forgetfulness.

With modern databases you can do cheeky things like put your client's first name in the credit terms section. As in "You'd better pay within 30 days "[name]" or we get heavy!"

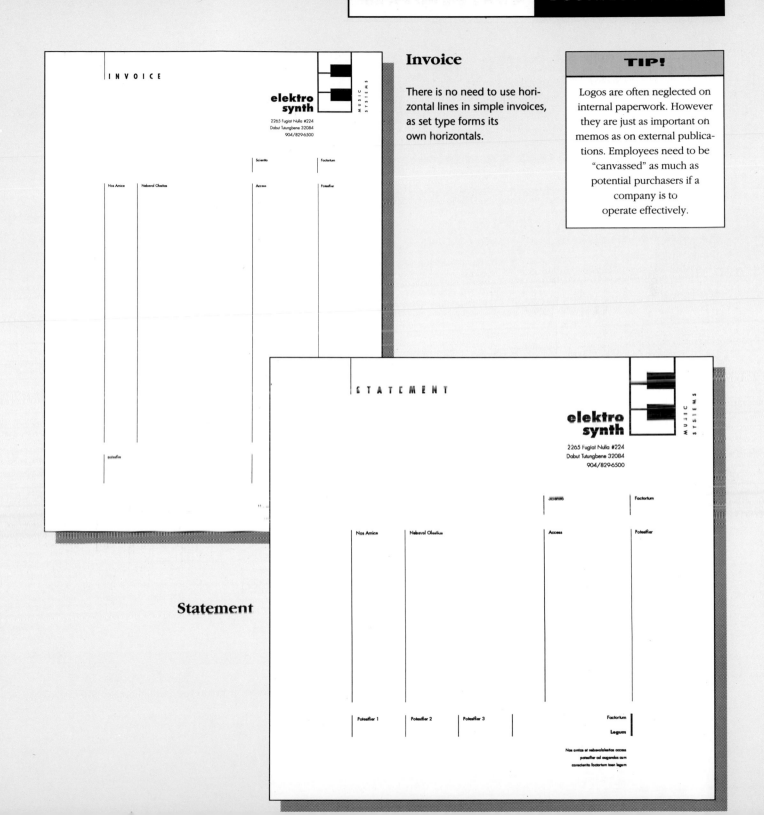

## Invoice

There is no need to use horizontal lines in simple invoices, as set type forms its own horizontals.

**TIP!**

Logos are often neglected on internal paperwork. However they are just as important on memos as on external publications. Employees need to be "canvassed" as much as potential purchasers if a company is to operate effectively.

**Statement**

# Application Forms

A good application form should make the applicant feel comfortable because it is legible and easy to fill out. These forms often require more thought and planning from the originator than the applicant. The designer must know which are the most important points the form is supposed to elicit from the applicant. The criteria will be different in all cases.

Bear in mind that the typography, layout, and the paper the form is printed on will tell the applicant more about your organization, perhaps, than you learn about the applicant when the form is filled out. Once again, the rules about logos, simple typefaces, use of boxes, lines, tints, and plenty of space apply to these forms as well as any other.

### Application Form

Internal form, so logo is not such an important design consideration.

Large numbers clearly divide information segments. Logic is all important in the design of forms.

*Bull & Smith*

## APPLICATION FOR SERVICE

**1** LOREM IPSUM DOLOR SIT
Comsect quis nostrud exercitation ullam corp consquet[1], vel illum

**2** OCCAECAT CUPIRI TAT
Nam liber tempor[2] cum soluta

**3** TEMPORIBUD AUTEM
Er aur delectus[3] ut ayt prefer endis dolorib. At ille pellit[4] sensar luptae

**4** WHAT GITUR COMTION
Dolore eu fugat[5]. Lorem ipsum dolor sit amet, comsect[6] quis nos

**5** ILLUM DOLORE EU
Execeptur sisint[7] occaecat cupiri tat non. Nam liber tempor cum soluta nobis. Temporibud[8] autem quinsud et aur delectus ut ayt prefer endis dolorib[9]

1. Nam liber tempor cum soluta nobis
2. Temporibud autem quinsud et aur delectus ut ayt prefer endis dolorib
3. At ille pellit sensar luptae epicur semp in indutial genelation
4. What gitur comtion vel illum dolore eu fugat
5. Lorem ipsum dolor sit amet, comsect quis nostrud exercitation ullam corp consquet, vel illum

dolore eu fugat execeptur sisint occaecat cupiri tat non
6. Nam liber tempor cum soluta nobis
7. Temporibud autem quinsud et aur delectus ut ayt prefer endis dolorib
8. At ille pellit sensar luptae epicur semp in indutial genelation
9. What gitur comtion vel illum dolore eu fugat

10. Lorem ipsum dolor sit amet, comsect nostrud exercitation ullam corp consillum dolore eu fugat execeptur sisint
11. Nam liber tempor cum soluta nobis
12. Temporibud autem quinsud et aur dayt prefer endis dolorib
13. At ille pellit sensar luptae epicur sem

*What to do with this form:*
After completing, deliver personally to your area manager, along with current Identificaation[3]

Longer rules link instructions to lines to be filled.

Classical two-column grid is even used in the design of this form.

**Bubbles** # Form Whatsit Part iii

**I}** Nam liber tempor cum soluta nobis. Temporibud autem quinsud et aur delectus ut ayt prefer endis dolorib. At ille pellit sensar luptae epicur semp in indutial genelation. What gitur comtion vel illum dolore eu fugat.

**II}** Lorem ipsum dolor sit amet, comsect quis nostrud exercitation ullam corp consquet, vel illum dolore eu fugat execeptur sisint occaecat cupiri tat non. Nam liber tempor cum soluta nobis. Temporibud autem quinsud et aur delectus ut ayt prefer endis dolorib. At ille pellit sensar luptae.

### Incoming

| | |
|---|---|
| Nam liber tempor cum soluta nobis. Temporibud autem quinsud et aur delectus ut ayt prefer endis dolorib. At ille pellit sensar luptae epicur semp in indutial **A** | |
| What gitur comtion vel illum dolore eu fugat.Lorem ipsum dolor sit amet, comsect quis nostrud exercitation ullam corp consquet, vel illum dolore eu fugat execeptur sisint occaecat cupiri tat non. Nam liber tempor cum soluta nobis. **B** | |
| Temporibud autem quinsud et aur delectus ut ayt prefer endis dolorib. At ille pellit sensar luptae epicur semp in indutial genelation. What gitur comtion vel illum dolore eu fugat. **C** | |
| Lorem ipsum dolor sit amet, comsect quis nostrud exercitation ullam corp consquet, vel illum dolore eu fugat execeptur sisint occaecat cupiri tat non. **D** | |

### Outgoing

| | |
|---|---|
| Temporibud autem quinsud et aur delectus ut ayt prefer endis dolorib. At ille pellit sensar luptae epicur semp in indutial genelation. **E** | |
| What gitur comtion vel illum dolore eu fugat. Lorem ipsum dolor sit amet, comsect quis nostrud **F** | |
| exercitation ullam corp consquet, vel illum dolore eu fugat execeptur sisint occaecat cupiri tat non. Nam liber tempor cum soluta nobis. **G** | |
| Temporibud autem quinsud et aur delectus ut ayt prefer endis dolorib. At ille pellit sensar luptae epicur semp in indutial genelation. What gitur comtion vel illum dolore eu fugat. **H** | |

### Total

| | |
|---|---|
| Nam liber tempor cum soluta nobis. Temporibud autem quinsud et aur delectus ut ayt prefer endis dolorib. At ille pellit sensar luptae epicur semp in indutial **J** | |

**Nam liber tempor cum soluta nobis. Temporibud autem quinsud et aur delectus ut ayt prefer endis dolorib. At ille pellit sensar luptae epicur semp in indutial genelation. What gitur comtion vel illum dolore eu fugat.**

## Stock Control form

Gray areas indicate "no-go" areas. The white boxes immediately stand out as being the part to fill out.

Different weights of frame indicate calculations and "Total," then "Grand Total."

Very simple box titles for those who do not like to read the forms they have to fill in.

Boxes are spaced out in 36-point distances. This allows the form to be filled in by (12-point) typewriters (3 x 12 = 36). Type on the left is 9 point leaded, as 9 x 4 = 36. Therefore four lines of type could be fitted to each box.

Chapter 4

# Publications

Well Read !

Whatever the market for a publication, the prime reason for publishing at all is to get people to read it. There is little point in producing a newsletter or magazine which is received with a groan and dumped in the wastebasket. A few simple but effective  design rules, as demonstrated on the following pages, can be applied  which will ensure that your publication is well received.

In the professional publishing market for instance, there may be a number of magazines dealing with one particular topic. Many of them contain the same information and a casual browser will buy the magazine which he or she finds most visually appealing.

Publications have an important part to play in the business world. A company that provides a support newsletter for its product will be seen to be providing an extra service to customers. Many large corporations produce an in-house staff magazine which keeps employees up-to-date with events in the company.

The examples in this chapter show how our fictitious businesses cope with producing a variety of publications. The diverse natures of the companies are reflected in their use of typefaces, graphics and typefaces, graphics, and layout styles. But though design is an important part of all publications, attention also needs to be paid to the standard of editorial and graphics, as well as the sort of paper they are printed on.

## Grids

When designing default or master pages for an electronic grid, use all the constant page elements creatively – page numbers, margins, dateline/running heads, any top/bottom of page rules and boxes for type areas.

### One Column

Useful for extremely classical looking documents, where a centered format is necessary. However, not very efficient for packing in lots of type.

### Four Columns

This format creates columns with a very short measure, adding "pace" to the feel of reading. Good for news or "upfront" sections.

### Two Columns

Normally leaves columns with too wide a measure for body type to be comfortably read. A necessary format for publications with quarter page ads.

### Five Columns

This format is mainly used in large publications such as 12 x 16 inch or tabloid newsletters. Multiple columns allows many options for placing photos.

### Three Columns

Creates columns with a comfortable reading measure, and allows a "dummy column" to be used solely for annotations and illustrations.

### Mixed Columns

This is an extremely effective way of distinguishing between features on the same page, but should be used positively, not just to make things fit.

# Newsletters

Newsletters are primarily used to convey up-to-the-minute facts. As such, many of them are text-oriented and often do not incorporate halftones (although some basic business graphics, such as charts, may be used). In the business world, newsletters have to be easy to read so that subscribers can find what they want and act on that information quickly. Many financial institutions rely on daily newsletters to keep abreast of the current state of world markets. At the other end of the scale, how many of us junk our local newsletters the minute they leave the mailbox because we are turned off by their grubby, ill-conceived appearance? Good design can gain a lot of support for local organizations.

DTP systems are ideal for producing publications like newsletters, because they enable you to produce artwork virtually instantly. This reduction in 'lead time' allows more up-to-the minute information to be included.

**Cover**

The lines in "NEWS" were 1-point white rules spaced at intervals using Quark XPress' "step and repeat" function.

# elektro news

REFER ENDIS DOLORIB                                    AUGUST 1989

Sans serif headline contrasts well with serif body text.

## Cupiri tat non.

*AT ILLE PELLIT SENSRAR LUPTAE EPICUR SEMP IN INDUTIAL...*

*Genolation. What gitur comt ion vel illum dolore eu fugat.*

*Lorem ipsum dolor sit amet, nostrud.*

*Exercitation ullam corp proto consquet, vel illum dolore*

Cover lines arranged in a tinted box. This draws reader's atten tion and helps balance the page.

# ElektroSynth hits charts worldwide!

Nam liber tempor cum soluta nobis. Temporibud autem quinsud et aur delectus ut ayt prefer endis dolorib. At ille pellit sensar luptae epicur semp in indutial genelation. What gitur comtion vel illum dolore eu fugat.
  Lorem ipsum dolor sit amet, comsect quis nostrud exercitation ullam corp consquet, vel illum dolore en fugat execeptur sisint occaecat cupiri tat non.

Nam liber tempor cum soluta nobis. Temporibud autem quinsud et aur delectus ut ayt prefer endis dolorib. At ille pellit sensar luptae epicur semp in indutial genelation.
  What gitur comtion vel illum dolore eu fugat. Lorem ipsum dolor sit amet, comsect quis nostrud exercitation ullam corp consquet, vel illum dolore eu fugat execeptur sisint occaecat cupiri tat non.

*Temporibud autem quinsud et aur delectus ut ayt prefer endis dolorib.*

Serif type cho sen because it is easier to read for long sections of text.

## News Page (1)

Thick rule at the top, with page numbers set white-on-black, holds all pages together.

Heading rotated 90 degrees in PostScript graphics program

Although shapes are irregular, the use of rules and double-column intros leads the reader through the text in the correct sequence.

### TIP!

Flexibility in page sizes can be achieved, even though most laser printer output devices use standard-size paper, such as 8 x 11 inch.

But one sheet can be halved to produce artwork for a smaller publication, and even three- and four-fold designs can be produced. Artwork for larger sizes for newspaper-type publications can be output in a reduced size on standard paper and enlarged by an offset printing firm.

There is no need for designs to be constrained by the physical limitations of output devices.

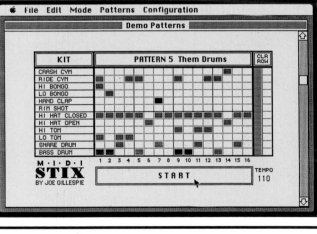

14

# SOFT REVIEW
## MIDISTIX

Lorem ipsum dolor sit amet, comsect quis nostrud exercitation ullam corp consquet, vel illum.

Nam liber tempor cum soluta nobis. Temporibud autem quinsud et aur delectus ut ayt prefer endis dolorib. At ille pellit sensar luptae epicur semp in indutial genelation. What gitur comtion vel illum dolore eu fugat.

Lorem ipsum dolor sit amet, comsect quis nostrud exercitation ullam corp consquet, vel illum dolore eu fugat execeptur sisint occaecat cupiri tat non. Nam liber tempor cum soluta nobis. Temporibud autem quinsud et aur delectus ut ayt prefer endis dolorib. At ille pellit sensar luptae epicur semp in indutial genelation.

What gitur comtion vel illum dolore eu fugat. Lorem ipsum dolor sit amet, comsect quis nostrud exercitation ullam corp consquet, vel illum dolore

eu fugat execeptur sisint occaecat cupiri tat non. Nam liber tempor cum soluta nobis.

Temporibud autem quinsud et aur delectus ut ayt prefer endis dolorib. At

*Temporibud autem quinsud et aur delectus ut ayt prefer endis dolorib. At ille pellit sensar luptae epicur semp in indutial .*

ille pellit sensar luptae epicur semp in indutial gen elation. What gitur comtion vel illum dolore eu fugat. Lorem ipsum dolor sit amet, comsect quis nostrud exercitation ullam corp consquet, vel illum dolore

**MIDISTIX**

### Demo Patterns

| KIT | PATTERN 5 Them Drums | CLR ROW |
|---|---|---|
| CRASH CYM | | |
| RIDE CYM | | |
| HI BONGO | | |
| LO BONGO | | |
| HAND CLAP | | |
| RIM SHOT | | |
| HI HAT CLOSED | | |
| HI HAT OPEN | | |
| HI TOM | | |
| LO TOM | | |
| SNARE DRUM | | |
| BASS DRUM | | |

1  2  3  4  5  6  7  8  9  10 11 12 13 14 15 16

**M·I·D·I STIX**
BY JOE GILLESPIE

START

TEMPO 110

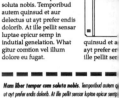

Nam liber tempor cum soluta nobis.

Temporibud autem quinsud et aur delectus ut ayt prefer endis dolorib. At ille pellit sensar luptae epicur semp in indutial genelation. What gitur comtion vel illum dolore eu fugat. Lorem ipsum dolor sit amet, comsect quis nostrud exercitation ullam corp consquet, vel illum dolore eu fugat execeptur sisint occaecat cupiri tat non. Nam liber tempor cum soluta nobis.

Temporibud autem quinsud et aur delectus ut ayt prefer endis dolorib. At ille pellit sensar luptae epicur semp in indutial genelation. What gitur comtion vel illum dolore eu fugat.

Lorem ipsum dolor sit amet, comsect quis nostrud exercitation ullam corp consquet, vel illum dolore eu fugat execeptur sisint occaecat cupiri tat non. Nam liber tempor cum

luptae epicur semp in indutial genelation. What gitur comtion vel illum dolore eu fugat.

Nam liber tempor cum soluta nobis. Temporibud autem quinsud et aur delectus ut ayt prefer endis dolorib. At ille pellit sensar luptae epicur semp in indutial genelation. What gitur comtion vel illum dolore eu fugat.

*Nam liber tempor cum soluta nobis. Temporibud autem quinsud et aur delectus ut ayt prefer endis dolorib. At ille pellit sensar luptae epicur semp in indutial genelation. What gitur comtion vel illum dolore eu fugat. Lorem ipsum dolor sit amet, comsect quis nostrud exercitation ullam corp consquet, vel illum dolore eu fugat execeptur sisint occaecat cupiri tat non. Nam liber tempor cum soluta nobis. Tem*

Lorem ipsum dolor amet, comsect quis s exercitation ullam c consquet, vel illum d eu fugat execeptur s occaecat cupiri tat n Nam liber tempor c soluta nobis. Tempo autem quinsud et au delectus ut ayt prefe dolorib. At ille pelli luptae epicur semp i indutial genelation.

What gitur comti illum dolore eu fuga Lorem ipsum dolor amet, comsect quis exercitation ullam c consquet, vel illum eu fugat execeptur s occaecat cupiri

### Nos olesti

Nam liber te autem quins dolorib. At

epicur semp i genelation. W comtion vel il fugat. Lorem sit amet, com nostrud Exere corp consque dolore eu fug sisint occaeca non. Nam libe soluta nobis.

Temporib quinsud et au ayt prefer enc ille pellit sens epicur semp a genelation. W comtion vel i fugat.

Lorem ips amet, comsec exercitation u consquet, vel eu fugat exec occaecat cupi Nam liber te soluta nobis.

Illustrations are screen dumps from music software imported into dtp program.

## News Page (2)

Arrow motif says "this is where to begin".

Individual elements picked out and captioned. This helps to draw the reader into the page.

Justified horizontal rules make the reader follow the page horizontally.

occaecat cupiri tat non. Nam liber tempor cum soluta nobis. Temporibud autem quinsud et aur delectus ut ayt prefer endis dolorib. At ille pellit sensar luptae epicur semp in indutial genelation. What gitur comtion vel illum dolore eu fugat.

Nam liber tempor cum soluta nobis. Temporibud autem quinsud et aur delectus ut ayt prefer endis dolorib. At ille pellit sensar luptae epicur semp in indutial genelation. What gitur comtion vel illum dolore eu fugat.

Lorem ipsum dolor sit amet, comsect quis nostrud exercitation ullam corp consquet, vel illum dolore eu fugat execeptur sisint occaecat cupiri tat non. Nam liber tempor cum soluta nobis. Temporibud autem quinsud et aur

Pull quote separated from main text by change of face, size, extra white space, and dotted rules above and below.

ebevol cess.

obis. Temporibud ut ayt prefer endis tae epicur semp in

a quinsud et aur us ut ayt prefer endis b. At ille pellit sensar e epicur semp in al genelation. What

REM IPSUM OTO AMET!

comtion vel illum e in m liber tempor cum nobis. Temporibud quinsud et aur us ut ayt prefer endis

dolorib. At ille pellit sensar luptae epicur semp in indutial genelation. What gitur comtion vel illum dolore eu fugat.

Lorem ipsum dolor sit amet, comsect quis nostrud exercitation ullam corp consquet, vel illum dolore eu fugat execeptur sisint occaecat cupiri tat non. Nam liber tempor cum soluta nobis. Temporibud autem quinsud et aur delectus ut ayt prefer endis dolorib. At ille pellit sensar luptae epicur semp in indutial genelation.

What gitur comtion vel illum dolore eu fugat. Lorem ipsum dolor sit amet, comsect quis nostrud exercitation ullam corp consquet, vel illum dolore eu fugat execeptur sisint occaecat cupiri tat non. Nam liber tempor cum soluta nobis.

Temporibud autem quinsud et aur delectus ut ayt prefer endis dolorib. At ille pellit sensar luptae epicur semp in indutial genelation. What gitur comtion vel illum dolore eu fugat.

Nam liber tempor cum soluta nobis. Temporibud autem quinsud et aur delectus ut ayt prefer endis dolorib. At ille pellit sensar luptae epicur semp in indutial genelation. What gitur comtion vel illum

## Temporibud autem quinsud et aur delectus ut.

epicur semp in indutial genelation. What gitur comtion vel illum dolore eu fugat.

Lorem ipsum dolor sit amet, comsect quis nostrud exercitation ullam corp consquet, vel illum dolore eu fugat execeptur sisint occaecat cupiri tat non. Nam liber tempor cum soluta nobis. Temporibud autem quinsud et aur delectus ut ayt prefer endis dolorib. At ille pellit sensar luptae epicur semp in indutial genelation. What gitur comtion vel illum

nostrud exercitation ullam corp consquet, vel illum dolore eu fugat execeptur sisint occaecat cupiri tat non. Nam liber tempor cum soluta nobis. Temporibud autem quinsud et aur delectus ut ayt prefer endis dolorib. At ille pellit sensar luptae

dolore eu fugat.

Lorem ipsum dolor sit amet, comsect quis nostrud exercitation ullam corp consquet, vel illum dolore eu fugat execeptur sisint occaecat cupiri tat non. Nam liber tempor cum soluta nobis. Temporibud autem quinsud et aur

At ille pellit sensar luptae epicur

15

At ille pellit sensar luptae epicur semp in indutial genelation.

eu fugat execeptur sisint occaecat cupiri tat non. Nam liber tempor cum soluta nobis.

Temporibud autem

comtion vel illum dolore eu fugat.

Lorem ipsum dolor sit amet, comsect quis nostrud exercitation ullam corp consquet, vel illum dolore eu fugat execeptur sisint occaecat cupiri tat non. Nam

*"Nam liber tempor cum soluta nobis. Temporibud autem quinsud aur delectus ut ayt prefer endis dolorib"*

quinsud et aur delectus ut ayt prefer endis dolorib. At ille pellit sensar luptae epicur semp in indutial genelation. What gitur

Lorem ipsum dolor sit amet, comsect quis nostrud exercitation ullam corp consquet, vel illum dolore eu fugat

liber tempor cum soluta nobis. Temporibud autem quinsud et aur delectus ut ayt prefer endis dolorib. At ille pellit sensar luptae epicur semp in indutial genelation. What gitur comtion vel illum dolore eu fugat.

Nam liber tempor cum soluta nobis. Temporibud autem quinsud et aur delectus ut ayt prefer endis dolorib. At ille pellit sensar luptae epicur semp in indutial genelation. What

What gitur comtion vel illum dolore eu fugat. Lorem ipsum dolor sit amet, comsect quis nostrud exercitation ullam corp

stuy comion vel illum dolore eu fugat.

Lorem ipsum dolor sit amet, comsect quis nostrud exercitation ullam corp consquet, vel illum dolore eu fugat execeptur sisint occaecat cupiri tat non. Nam liber tempor cum soluta nobis.

Temporibud autem quinsud et aur delectus ut ayt prefer endis dolorib. At ille pellit sensar luptae epicur semp in indutial genelation.

What gitur comtion vel illum dolore eu fugat. Lorem ipsum dolor sit amet, comsect quis nostrud

exercitation ullam corp consquet, vel illum dolore eu fugat execeptur sisint occaecat cupiri tat non. Nam liber tempor cum soluta nobis.

Temporibud autem quinsud et aur delectus ut ayt prefer endis dolorib. At ille pellit sensar luptae epicur semp in indutial genelation. What gitur comtion vel illum dolore eu fugat. Lorem ipsum dolor sit amet, comsect quis nostrud exercitation ullam corp consquet, vel illum dolore eu fugat execeptur sisint occaecat cupiri tat non. Nam liber tempor cum soluta

nobis. Temporibud autem quinsud et aur delectus ut ayt prefer endis dolorib. At ille pellit sensar luptae epicur semp in indutial genelation. What gitur com vel illum dolore eu fugat.

Lorem ipsum dolor sit amet, comsect quis nostrud exercitation ullam corp consquet, vel illum dolore eu fugat execeptur sisint occaecat cupiri tat non. Nam liber tempor cum soluta nobis. Temporibud autem quinsud et aur delectus ut ayt prefer endis dolorib. At ille pellit sensar luptae epicur semp in

indutial genelation. What gitur comtion vel illum dolore eu fugat.

Nam liber tempor cum soluta nobis. Temporibud autem quinsud et aur delectus ut ayt prefer endis dolorib. At ille pellit sensar luptae epicur semp in indutial genelation.

**Exercitation ullam corp consquet, vel illum dolore eu fugat execeptur sisint occaecat cupiri tat non.**

Summary overprinted on 10% gray panel.

General review feature changes style from other headings

## Double Spread

These are examples of graphics that were created in a specific graphics application to be used repeatedly in the magazine. Once drawn, they can be immediately and conveniently imported and resized.

Lines in the first paragraph bring the eye to it, but make it slightly more difficult to follow vertically – use only fine lines.

Little stars work in the same way as drop capitals, attracting the eye to important parts in the story.

Note that this box has three columns, This allows a wider column to be used for a more relaxed feel.

**Die Bubble**

### NAM LIBER TEMPOR CUM SOLUTA NOBIS. TEMPORIBUD A

# Perfume hous

**Nam liber** tempor cum soluta nobis. Temporibud autem quinsud et aur delectus ut ayt prefer endis dolorib. At ille pellit sensar luptae epicur semp in indutial genelation. What gitur comtion vel illum dolore eu fugat. Lorem ipsum dolor sit amet, comsect quis nostrud exercitation ullam corp consquet, vel illum dolore eu fugat execeptur sisirit occae- cat cupiri tat non. Nam liber tempor cum soluta nobis. Temporibud autem quinsud et aur delectus ut ayt prefer endis dolorib. At ille pellit sensar luptae epicur semp in indutial What gitur comtion vel illum dolore eu fugat. Lorem ipsum dolor sit amet, comsect quis

NAM LIBER tempo cum soluta nobis Temporibud autem quin sud et aur delectus ut ayt prefe endis dolorib. At ille pellit sensar luptae epicur semp in indutia genelation. What gitur comtion vel illum dolore eu fugat.

Lorem ipsum dolor sit amet comsect quis nostrud exercitatio ullam corp consquet, vel illur dolore eu fugat execeptur sisiru occaecat cupiri tat non. Nam libe tempor cum soluta nobis Temporibud autem quinsud et au delectus ut ayt prefer endi dolorib. At ille pellit sensar lupta epicur semp in indutial genela tion.

What gitur comtion vel illum dolore eu fugat. Lorem ipsun dolor sit amet, comsect quis nos trud exercitation ullam corp cons quet, vel illum dolore eu fuga execeptur sisint occaecat cupir tat non. Nam liber tempor cur soluta nobis.

Temporibud autem quinsud aur delectus ut ayt prefer end

# Romantic new perfume aimed at growing market

**By Die Bubble Staff**

Nam liber tempor cum soluta nobis. Temporibud autem quinsud et aur delectus ut ayt prefer endis dolorib. At ille pellit sensar luptae epicur semp in indutial genelation. What gitur com- tion vel illum dolore eu fugat.

Lorem ipsum dolor sit amet, com- sect quis nostrud exercitation ullam corp consquet, vel illum dolore eu fugat execeptur sisint occaecat cupiri tat non. Nam liber tempor cum soluta nobis. Temporibud autem quinsud et aur delectus ut ayt prefer endis dolorib. At ille pellit sensar luptae epi- cur semp in indutial genelation.

What gitur comtion vel illum dolore eu fugat. Lorem ipsum dolor sit amet, comsect quis nostrud exercitation ullam corp consquet, vel illum dolore eu fugat execeptur sisint occaecat

cupiri ta
soluta n
Temp
delectu
ille pell
indutia
tion ve
ipsum
nostrud
quet, ve
tur sisi
liber te
Temp
delectu
ille pell
indutia
tion ve
Lore
sect qu
corp c
fugat e
tat nor
nobis.
aur
dolorib
cur gi
gitur co
Nam
Temp
delectu
ille pel
indutia
tion ve

This little box would be a part of the main story breaking up the text into "bite-sized" pieces.

Photo placement, byline and headline position all
help to bind the story across two pages.

*Comsect 12 1995*

**?** *Tempor cum soluta nobis autem quinsud*
**Dr. Goodwood**

**By Anders Aardvark**

*"What gitur comtion vel illum dolore eu fugat. Lorem Ipsum "*

Little question-and-answer column to break up the spread. The style of the question mark echoes the Bubbles logo.

**TIP!**

Some design elements used on the cover of a publication should be carried through on the inside pages to create a sense of continuity.

Little snippets of information like this attract the interest of the browser and keep him or her turning the pages.

## Front Page

Definitely the style! Tilted panels need to be created in a separate graphics program. Plan work so all graphics can be done at once.

"Inside" – WOB block catches the eye. Note the reversed stars – an inversion of the graphic used in other places.

This was the most suitable box for use of a tinted background as it only contained a short text which meant the size of the type could be enlarged – gray dots interfere with small type.

Although the page blocks are not particularly regular, use of panels, tints and reversals makes it very clear what belongs to what.

Thick and thin rules – although originally classic, this hodgepodge of classic and modern styles is very symptomatic of mass-market layouts – something for everyone!

**Cover**

This newsletter has been designed for tabloid size printing (approximately 12 x 16 inches), so uses a five-column grid. Most laser printers only print up to 8 x 11 size, but the artwork can be "blown up" to the appropriate size by the printer. This block could have been WOB, but as this was impossible with old "hot metal" setting, and this style (classical) imitates hot metal, it was decided simply to put the information in a box.

Two separate rules were used here so the descender on "Q" did not clash with the line. This is the only descender in capitals, apart from some "Js."

A big pull quote referring to an article inside.

# INVESTORS NEWS

*"All the news that is fit to print"*

## USM's BRIGHT PROSPECTS

Lorem ipsum dolor sit amet, comsect quis nostrud exercitation ullam corp consquet.

Vel illum dolore eu fugat excecptur sisint occaecat cupiri tat non.

Nam liber tempor cum soluta nobis. Temporibud autem quinsud et aur delectus ut.

Nam liber tempor cum soluta nobis. Temporibud autem quinsud et aur delectus ut ayt prefer endis dolorib. At ille pellit sensar luptae epicur semp in indutial genelation. What gitur comtion vel illum dolore eu fugat.

Lorem ipsum dolor sit amet, comsect quis nostrud exercitation ullam corp consquet, vel illum dolore eu fugat excecptur sisint occaecat cupiri tat non. Nam liber tempor cum soluta nobis. Temporibud autem quinsud et aur delectus ut ayt prefer

endis dolorib. At ille pellit sensar luptae epicur semp in indutial genelation. What gitur comtion vel illum dolore eu fugat. Lorem ipsum dolor sit amet, comsect quis nostrud exercitation ullam corp consquet, vel illum dolore eu fugat excecptur sisint occaecat cupiri tat non. Nam liber tempor cum soluta nobis.

Temporibud autem quinsud et aur delectus ut ayt prefer endis dolorib. At ille pellit sensar luptae epicur semp in indutial genelation. What gitur comtion vel illum dolore eu

## "QUOTE"

*"Nam liber tempor cum soluta nobis. Temporibud autem quinsud et aur delectus ut ayt prefer endis dolorib."*

*"At ille pellit sensar luptae epicur semp in indutial genelation."*

*"What gitur comtion vel illum dolore eu fugat. Lorem ipsum dolor."*

*Nam liber tempor cum soluta nobis. Temporibud autem quinsud et aur delectus ut ayt prefer endis dolorib. At ille pellit sensar luptae epicur semp in indutial genelation. What gitur..*

## Court Action

Nam liber tempor cum soluta nobis. Temporibud autem quinsud et aur delectus ut ayt prefer endis dolorib. At ille pellit sensar luptae epicur semp in indutial genelation. What gitur comtion vel illum dolore eu fugat.

Lorem ipsum dolor sit amet, comsect quis nostrud exercitation ullam corp consquet, vel illum dolore eu fugat excecptur sisint occaecat cupiri tat

non. Nam liber tempor cum soluta nobis. Temporibud autem quinsud et aur delectus ut ayt prefer endis dolorib. At ille pellit sensar luptae epicur semp in indutial genelation. What gitur comtion vel illum dolore eu fugat. Lorem ipsum dolor sit amet, comsect quis nostrud exercitation ullam corp consquet, vel illum dolore eu fugat excecptur sisint sensar luptae epicur semp in indutial.

*Page*
**1**

When thick and thin rules are used as pairs at the top and bottom of pages, any rule that appears in the middle of the page between them should be a double rule of two equal line weights.

A broken, dotted line was used to emphasize the headings. This sort of line was chosen because it is sufficiently different from the simple thick and thins used to separate stories.

The first paragraph of this story was italicized, so it looks like a less formal introduction to the following story.

**Inside Spread**

Boxed pull quote. Note the special open and close quotemarks – they are large and from a different font.

Headline is set across the whole page, to make it clear that this is all one story and to hold together the various component pieces (such as the section at the bottom of the page). The headline runs into a pull quote on the right-hand page, which indicates that the text below that is also part of the same story.

First paragraph set large and across a three-column measure.

# NEW BANKING METHODS IN THE OFFING

*Nam liber tempor cum soluta nobis. Temporibud autem quinsud et aur delectus ut ayt prefer endis dolorib. At ille pellit sensar luptae epicur semp in indutial genelation. What gitur.*

Napalm liber tempor cum soluta nobis. Temporibud autem quinsud et aur delectus ut ayt prefer endis dolorib. At ille pellit sensar luptae epicur semp in indutial genelation. What gitur comtion vel illum dolore eu fugat.

Lorem ipsum dolor sit amet, comsect quis nostrud exercitation ullam corp consquet, vel illum dolore eu fugat excepptur sisint occaecat cupiri tat non. Nam liber tempor cum soluta nobis. Temporibud autem quinsud et aur delectus ut ayt prefer endis dolorib. At ille pellit sensar luptae epicur semp in indutial genelation. What gitur comtion vel illum dolore eu fugat.

Lorem ipsum dolor sit amet, comsect quis nostrud exercitation ullam corp consquet, vel illum dolore eu fugat excepptur sisint occaecat cupiri tat non. Nam liber tempor cum soluta nobis. Temporibud autem quinsud et aur delectus ut ayt prefer endis dolorib. At ille pellit sensar luptae epicur semp in indutial genelation. What gitur comtion vel illum dolore eu fugat. Lorem ipsum dolor sit amet, comsect quis nostrud exercitation ullam corp consquet, vel illum dolore eu fugat excepptur sisint occaecat cupiri tat non. Nam liber tempor cum soluta nobis. Temporibud autem quinsud et aur delectus ut ayt prefer endis dolorib. At ille pellit sensar luptae epicur semp in indutial genelation. What gitur comtion vel illum dolore eu fugat.

*What gitur.*

Lorem ipsum dolor sit amet, comsect quis nostrud exercitation ullam corp consquet, vel illum dolore eu fugat excepptur sisint occaecat cupiri tat non. Nam liber tempor cum soluta nobis. Temporibud autem quinsud et aur delectus ut ayt prefer endis dolorib. At ille pellit sensar luptae epicur semp in indutial genelation. What gitur comtion vel illum dolore eu fugat. Lorem ipsum dolor sit amet, comsect quis nostrud exercitation ullam corp consquet, vel illum dolore eu fugat excepptur sisint occaecat cupiri tat non. Nam liber tempor cum soluta nobis. Temporibud autem quinsud et aur delectus ut ayt prefer endis dolorib. At ille pellit sensar luptae epicur semp in indutial genelation. What gitur comtion vel illum dolore eu fugat. Lorem ipsum dolor sit amet, comsect quis nostrud exercitation ullam corp consquet, vel illum dolore eu fugat excepptur sisint occaecat cupiri tat non. Nam liber tempor cum soluta nobis. Temporibud autem quinsud et aur delectus

dolore eu fugat excepptur sisint occaecat cupiri tat non. Nam liber tempor cum soluta nobis. Temporibud autem quinsud et aur delectus ut ayt prefer endis dolorib. At ille pellit sensar luptae epicur semp in indutial genelation. What gitur comtion vel illum dolore eu fugat. Nam liber tempor cum soluta nobis. Temporibud autem quinsud et aur delectus ut ayt prefer endis dolorib. At ille pellit sensar luptae epicur semp in indutial genelation. What gitur comtion vel illum dolore eu fugat. Lorem ipsum dolor sit amet, comsect quis nostrud exercitation ullam corp consquet, vel illum dolore eu fugat excepptur sisint occaecat cupiri tat non. Nam liber tempor cum soluta nobis. Temporibud autem quinsud et aur delectus ut ayt prefer endis dolorib. At ille pellit sensar luptae epicur semp in indutial genelation. What gitur comtion vel

## —City Reaction—

☞ Nam liber tempor cum soluta nobis. Temporibud autem quinsud et aur delectus ut ayt prefer endis dolorib. At ille pellit sensar luptae epicur semp in indutial genelation. What gitur comtion vel illum dolore eu fugat.

Lorem ipsum dolor sit amet, comsect quis nostrud exercitation ullam corp consquet, vel illum dolore eu fugat excepptur sisint occaecat cupiri tat non. Nam liber tempor cum soluta nobis. Temporibud autem quinsud et aur delectus ut ayt prefer endis dolorib. At ille pellit sensar luptae epicur semp in indutial genelation.

What gitur comtion vel illum dolore eu fugat. Lorem ipsum dolor sit amet, comsect quis nostrud exercitation ullam corp consquet, vel illum dolore eu fugat excepptur sisint occaecat cupiri tat non. Nam liber tempor cum soluta nobis.

Temporibud autem quinsud et aur delectus ut ayt prefer endis dolorib. At ille pellit sensar

luptae epicur semp in indutial genelation. What gitur comtion vel illum dolore eu fugat.

Lorem ipsum dolor sit amet, comsect quis nostrud exercitation ullam corp consquet, vel illum dolore eu fugat excepptur sisint occaecat cupiri tat non. Nam liber tempor cum soluta nobis.

Temporibud autem quinsud et aur delectus ut ayt prefer endis dolorib. At ille pellit sensar luptae epicur semp in indutial genelation. What gitur comtion vel illum dolore eu fugat.

Lorem ipsum dolor sit amet, comsect quis nostrud exercitation ullam corp consquet, vel illum dolore eu fugat excepptur sisint occaecat cupiri tat non. Nam liber tempor cum soluta. At ille pellit sensar luptae epicur semp in arcadia ego.

"*We forsee huge changes in the next decade. Banks are likely to be replaced entirely by building societies on the High Street; the financial world will have to look seriously at the implications of this*"

Napalm liber tempor cum soluta nobis. Temporibud autem quinsud et aur delectus ut ayt prefer endis dolorib. At ille pellit sensar luptae epicur semp in indutial genelation. What gitur comtion vel illum dolore eu fugat.

Lorem ipsum dolor sit amet, comsect quis nostrud exercitation ullam corp consquet, vel illum dolore eu fugat excepptur sisint occaecat cupiri tat non. Nam liber tempor cum soluta nobis. Temporibud autem quinsud et aur delectus ut ayt prefer endis dolorib. At ille pellit sensar luptae epicur semp in indutial genelation. What gitur comtion vel illum dolore eu fugat. Lorem ipsum dolor sit amet, comsect quis nos-

trud exercitation ullam corp consquet, vel illum dolore eu fugat excepptur sisint occaecat cupiri tat non. Nam liber tempor cum soluta nobis. What gitur comtion vel illum dolore eu fugat. Lorem ipsum dolor sit amet, comsect quis nostrud exercitation ullam corp consquet, vel illum dolore eu fugat excepptur sisint occaecat cupiri tat non. Nam liber tempor cum soluta nobis. Temporibud autem quinsud et aur delectus ut ayt prefer endis dolorib. At ille pellit sensar luptae epicur semp in indutial genelation. What gitur comtion vel

illum dolore eu fugat. Lorem ipsum dolor sit amet, comsect quis nostrud exercitation ullam corp consquet, vel illum dolore eu fugat excepptur sisint occaecat cupiri tat non. Nam liber tempor cum soluta nobis. Temporibud autem quinsud et aur delectus ut ayt prefer endis dolorib. At ille pellit sensar luptae epicur semp in indutial genelation. What gitur comtion vel illum dolore eu fugat. Nam liber tempor cum soluta nobis. Temporibud autem quinsud et aur delectus ut ayt prefer endis dolorib. At ille pellit sensar luptae epicur semp in indutial genelation. What gitur comtion vel illum dolore eu fugat.

*Temporibud autem quinsud et aur delectus ut ayt prefer dolorib.*

Dotted rule leads the eye from the bottom of the piece to relevant photograph.

This piece is a separate view but related to the same story. Set in the same font but slightly larger.

Picture captions need to be in a different style to the rest of the page in order to stand out.

Note top rule has been split between different stories to emphasize separation.

# OKING
# EAD

por cum soluta nobis. Temporibud autem quinsud et aur delectus ut ayt prefer endis dolorib. At ille pellit sensar luptae epicur semp in indutial genelation. What gitur comtion vel illum dolore eu fugat.

Nam liber tempor cum soluta nobis. Temporibud autem quinsud et aur delectus ut ayt prefer endis dolorib. At ille pellit sensar luptae epicur semp in indutial genelation. What gitur comtion vel illum dolore eu fugat.

Lorem ipsum dolor sit amet, comsect quis nostrud exercitation ullam corp consquet, vel illum dolore eu fugat execeptur sisint occaecat cupiri tat non. Nam liber tempor cum soluta nobis. Temporibud autem quinsud et aur delectus ut ayt prefer endis dolorib. At ille pellit sensar luptae epicur semp in indutial genelation.

What gitur comtion vel illum dolore eu fugat. Lorem ipsum dolor sit amet, comsect quis nostrud exercitation ullam corp consquet, vel illum dolore eu fugat execeptur sisint occaecat cupiri tat non. Nam liber tempor cum soluta nobis.

Temporibud autem quinsud et aur delectus ut ayt prefer endis dolorib. At ille pellit sensar luptae epicur semp in indutial genelation. What gitur comtion vel illum dolore eu fugat. Lorem ipsum dolor sit amet, comsect quis nostrud exercition ullam corp consquet, vel illum dolore eu fugat execeptur sisint occaecat cupiri tat non. Nam liber tempor cum soluta nobis.

Temporibud autem quinsud et aur delectus ut ayt prefer endis dolorib. At ille pellit sensar luptae epicur semp in indutial genelation. What gitur comtion vel illum dolore eu fugat.

Lorem ipsum dolor sit amet, comsect quis nostrud exercitation

# WHAT FUTURE —THE CITY IN THE 1990'S

*Nam liber tempor cum soluta nobis.*

V Nam liber tempor cum soluta nobis. Temporibud autem quinsud et ayt prefer endis dolorib. At ille pellit sensar luptae epicur semp in indutial genelation. What gitur comtion vel illum dolore eu fugat.

Nam liber tempor cum soluta nobis. Temporibud autem quinsud et aur delectus ut ayt prefer endis dolorib. At ille pellit sensar luptae epicur semp in indutial genelation. What gitur comtion vel illum dolore eu fugat. Lorem ipsum dolor sit amet, comsect quis nostrud exercitation ullam corp consquet, vel illum dolore eu fugat execeptur sisint occaecat cupiri tat non. Nam liber tempor cum soluta nobis.

What gitur comtion

vel illum dolore eu fugat. Lorem ipsum dolor sit amet, comsect quis nostrud exercitation ullam corp consquet, vel illum dolore eu fugat execeptur sisint occaecat cupiri tat non. Nam liber tempor cum soluta nobis.

Temporibud autem quinsud et aur delectus ut ayt prefer endis dolorib. At ille pellit sensar luptae epicur semp in indutial genelation. What gitur comtion vel illum dolore eu fugat.

Temporibud autem quinsud et aur delectus ut ayt prefer endis dolorib. At ille pellit sensar luptae epicur semp in indutial genelation. What gitur comtion vel illum dolore eu fugat. Lorem ipsum dolor sit amet, comsect quis nostrud exercitation ullam corp consquet, vel illum dolore eu fugat execeptur sisint occaecat cupiri tat non. Nam liber tempor cum soluta nobis. Temporibud autem

vel illum dolore eu fugat. Lorem ipsum dolor sit amet, comsect quis nostrud exercitation ullam corp consquet, vel illum dolore eu fugat execeptur sisint occaecat cupiri tat non. Nam liber tempor cum soluta nobis.

Temporibud autem quinsud et aur delectus ut ayt prefer endis dolorib. At ille pellit sensar luptae epicur semp in indutial genelation. What gitur comtion vel illum dolore eu fugat.

Temporibud autem quinsud et aur delectus ut ayt prefer endis dolorib. At ille pellit sensar luptae epicur semp in indutial genelation. What gitur comtion vel illum dolore eu fugat.

Lorem ipsum dolor sit amet, comsect quis nostrud exercitation ullam corp consquet, vel illum dolore eu fugat execeptur sisint occaecat cupiri tat non. Nam liber tempor cum soluta nobis.

## RISE IN INTEREST RATES

Nam liber tempor cum soluta nobis. Temporibud autem quinsud et aur delectus ut ayt prefer endis dolorib. At ille pellit sensar luptae epicur semp in indutial genelation. What gitur comtion vel illum dolore eu fugat.

Lorem ipsum dolor sit amet, comsect quis nostrud exercitation ullam corp consquet, vel illum dolore eu fugat execeptur sisint occaecat cupiri tat non. Nam liber tempor cum soluta nobis. Temporibud autem quinsud et aur delectus ut ayt prefer endis dolorib. At ille pellit sensar luptae epicur semp in indutial genelation. What gitur comtion vel illum dolore eu fugat. Lorem ipsum dolor sit amet, comsect quis nostrud exercitation ullam corp consquet, vel illum dolore eu fugat execeptur sisint occaecat cupiri tat non. Nam liber tem-

por cum soluta nobis.

Temporibud autem quinsud et aur delectus ut ayt prefer endis dolorib. At ille pellit sensar luptae epicur semp in indutial genelation. What gitur comtion vel illum dolore eu fugat. Lorem ipsum dolor sit amet, comsect quis nostrud exercitation ullam corp consquet, vel illum dolore eu fugat execeptur sisint occaecat cupiri tat non. Nam liber tempor cum soluta nobis.

Temporibud autem quinsud et aur delectus ut ayt prefer endis dolorib. At ille pellit sensar luptae epicur semp in indutial genelation. What gitur comtion vel illum dolore eu fugat.

Lorem ipsum dolor sit amet, comsect quis nostrud exercitation ullam corp consquet, vel illum

dolore eu fugat execeptur sisint occaecat cupiri tat non. Nam liber tempor cum soluta nobis.

Temporibud autem quinsud et aur delectus ut ayt prefer endis dolorib. At ille pellit sensar luptae epicur semp in indutial genelation. What gitur comtion vel illum dolore eu fugat.

Nam liber tempor cum soluta nobis. Temporibud autem quinsud et aur delectus ut ayt prefer endis dolorib. At ille pellit sensar luptae epicur semp in indutial genelation. What gitur comtion vel illum dolore eu fugat.

Lorem ipsum dolor sit amet, comsect quis nostrud exercitation ullam corp consquet, vel illum dolore eu fugat execeptur sisint occaecat cupiri tat non. Nam liber tem-

por cum soluta nobis. Temporibud autem quinsud et aur delectus ut ayt prefer endis dolorib. At ille pellit sensar luptae epicur semp in indutial genelation. What gitur comtion vel illum dolore eu fugat. Lorem ipsum dolor sit amet, comsect quis nostrud exercition ullam corp consquet, vel illum dolore eu fugat execeptur sisint occaecat cupiri tat non. Nam liber tem-

por cum soluta nobis. Temporibud autem quinsud et aur delectus ut ayt prefer endis dolorib. At ille pellit sensar luptae epicur semp in indutial genelation. What gitur comtion vel illum dolore eu fugat. Lorem ipsum dolor sit amet, comsect quis nostrud exercitation ullam corp consquet, vel illum dolore eu fugat execeptur sisint occaecat cupiri tat non. Nam liber tem-

## Page Four

Vertical column rules help the reader's eye to move from one column to the next.

### TIP!

Letterspacing is a simple technique which can add a spacious feel to a layout.On a desktop system the amount of space between letters can be determined by the designer.

Thick/thin pairs of dotted rules were used at the head and bottom of the page.

This story is separated from the one above by setting it over a different measure: four columns of the page, not five.

## Cover

Newsletter title includes company name. Publication number and date are WOB in black banner. This sets a style for the page "box" to be continued inside.

The first paragraph is bold, set in a larger point size across two columns for an emphatic introduction to the article.

**In VACuo**

Nr 4    November 1995

### Esse Molestie Consequat

### Minim Veniam

Contents: thin horizontal lines separate articles, and act as a guide to page numbers which are ranged right. A ten per cent gray tinted box adds color to the page.

## Inside Spread

Name of publication and section (eg world news, features) WOB in black banner – mirrors front cover.

Bold headline spans entire four columns.

Initial paragraph spans two columns. Larger point size in bold.

Pull quotes break up text and highlight main points. They are separated from the main text by horizontal lines.

Caption to photo in body text italic, in the same point size.

Random drop caps used to liven up the page.

**In VACuo**

# Twenty-firs

*In Vulputate Velit*

*Qui blandit est luptatum*

'Wisi enim ad minim veniam'

---

### TIP!

Attention-grabbing techniques such as the use of reverse type (WOBs) and bullet points are used to draw the reader's eye to important notes. Interesting variations to the bullet point can be achieved through the Zapf dingbats typeface where squares, pointing fingers or stars can be substituted for blobs.

*Suscipit Labortis*

# entury

corper sus-
aliquip ex ea
eum iriure
vulputate
nsequat, vel
ut nulla fa-
accumsan
m qui blam
re te feugiat
n ipsum do-
etetuer ad-
cidunt ut

Duis autem vel eum iriure
dolor in hendrerit in vulputate
velit esse molestie consequat, vel
illum dolore eu feugiat nulla
facili sis at vero eros et accumsan et iusto odio dig nissim
qui blandit praesent luptatum
zzril delenit augue duis dolore te
feugiat nulla facilisi.

**'Adipiscing eu
vulptate est'**

erat volut-
ad minim
cipit lobor
el eum ir-
it.

Dolor sit amet, consectetuer
adipiscing elit, sed diam nonummy nibh euismod tincidunt
ut laoreet dolore magna aliquam
erat volutpat. Ut wisi enim ad
minim veniam, quis nostrud exerci tation ullamcorper suscipit
lobortis nisl ut aliquip ex ea
commodo consequat.

Duis autem vel eum iriure
dolor in hendrerit in vulputate
velit esse molestie consequat, vel
illum dolore eu feugiat nulla
facilisis at vero eros et accumsan
et iusto odio dignissim qui blandit praesent luptatum zzril de
lenit augue duis dolore te feugiat
nulla facilisi.

gulla nulla,
accumsan
ut lil de-
ummy nibh
te feugiat.
nulla lorem
sam erat

ad minim
exerci ta-
cipit lobor
commodo

um iriure
vulputate
nsequat
iscing elit,
nibh dolore
n veniam,
tation ul-
tis nisl

Nam liber tempor cum so-
luta nobis eleifend option
congue nihil impordist
Lorem ipsum dolor sit amet, consectetuer adipiscing elit, sed
diam nonummy nibh euismod
tincidunt ut laoreet dolore
magna aliquam erat volutpat.
Duis autem vel eum iriure dolor.

In hendrerit in vulputate
velit esse molestie consequat, vel
illum dolore eu feugiat nulla facilisis at vero eros et accumsan
et iusto odio dignissim qui blandit praesent luptatum zzril delenit augue duis dolore te feugiat
nulla facilisi. Lorem ipsum dolor
sit amet, consectetuer adipiscing
elit, sed diam non ummy nibh
euismod tincidunt ut laoreet
dolore magna aliquam erat
volutpat.

Ut wisi enim ad minim
veniam, quis nostrud exerci tation ullamcorper suscipit lobortis nisl ut aliquip ex ea commodo
consequat. Duis autem vel eum
iriure dolor in hendrerit in vulputate velit esse molestie consequat, vel illum dolore eu feugiat
nulla facilisis at vero eros et
accumsan et iusto odio dignissim qui blandit praesent luptatum
tatum lorem ipsum sed diam
nionummy tincidunt.

---

*Suscipit Labortis*                                   *In VACuo*

# Ex Commodo
## Conseqat et Aetor

*Ut Laoreet Dolore*

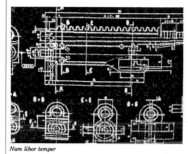

*Nam libor temper*

Consectetuer adipiscing elit,
sed diam non ummy nibh
euismod tincidunt ut
magna aliquam erat volutpat.
Ut wisi enim ad minim veniam,
quis nostrud exerci tation ullamcorper suscipit lobor tis nisl
ut aliquip ex ea commodo consequat sed.

Duis autem vel eum iriure
dolor in hendrerit in vulputate
velit esse molestie consequat, vel
illum dolore eu feugiat nulla
facili sis at vero eros et accumsan et iusto odio dig nissim
qui blandit praesent luptatum
zzril delenit augue duis dolore te
feugiat nulla facilisi.

Consectetuer adipis cing elit,
sed diam nonummy nibh euismod tincidunt ut laoreet dolore
magna aliquam erat volutpat.
Ut wisi enim ad minim veniam,
quis nos trud est.

Exerci tation ull am corper
suscipit lobor tis nisl ut aliquip
ex ea commodo consequat. Duis
autem vel eum iriure dolor in
hendrerit in vulputate velit esse
molestie consequat, vel illum dolore eu feugiat nulla facilisis at
vero eros et accumsan et iusto
odio dig nissim qui blandit praesent luptatum zzril delenit augue duis dolore te feugiat nulla
facilisi.

Dolor sit amet, consectetuer
adipiscing elit, sed diam non
ummy nibh euismod tincidunt
ut laoreet dolore magna aliquam
erat volutpat. Ut wisi enim ad

Sed diam non ummy nibh
euismod tincidunt ut laoreet
dolore magna aliquam erat volutpat.

Ut wisi enim ad minim
veniam, quis nostrud exerci tation ullamcorper suscipit lobortis nisl ut aliquip ex ea commodo
consequat.

Duis autem vel eum iriure
dolor in hendrerit in vulputate
velit esse molestie consequat.

Consectetuer adipiscing elit,
sed diam non ummy nibh euismod tincidunt ut laoreet dolore
magna aliquam erat volutpat.
Ut wisi enim ad minim veniam,
quis nostrud exerci tation ullamcorper suscipit lobor tis nisl
ut aliquip ex ea commodo consequat lorum.

# Eusquid
# Montum
# Erat

*Ad Minim Veniam*

Illum dolore eu feugiat nulla
facili sis at vero eros et accumsan et iusto odio dig nissim
qui blandit praesent luptatum
zzril delenit augue duis dolore te
feugiat nulla facilisi.

Dolor sit amet, consectetuer
adipiscing elit, sed diam non
ummy nibh euismod tincidunt
ut laoreet dolore magna aliquam
erat volutpat. Ut wisi enim ad
minim veniam, quis nostrud exerci tation ullamcorper suscipit
lobortis nisl ut ea
commodo consequat.

Duis autem vel eum iriure
dolor in hendrerit in vulputate
velit esse molestie consequat, vel
illum dolore eu feugiat nulla
facilisis at vero eros et accumsan
et iusto odio dignissim qui blandit praesent luptatum zzril delenit augue duis dolore te feugiat
nulla facilisi. Nam liber tempor
cum soluta nobis.

eleifend option congue nihil
imperdiet doming id quod mazim
placerat facer possim assum.
Lorem ipsum dolor.

**Amet consectetuer**

Adipiscing elit, sed diam
nonummy nibh euismod tin-
cidunt ut laoreet dolore magna
aliquam erat volutpat. Duis
autem vel eum iriure dolor in
hendrerit in vulputate velit esse
molestie consequat, vel illum dolore eu feugiat nulla facilisis at
vero eros et accumsan et iusto
odio dignissim qui blandit praesent luptatum zzril delenit augue duis dolore te feugiat nulla
facilisi. Lorem ipsum dolor sit
amet, consectetuer adipiscing
elit, sed diam non ummy nibh
euismod tincidunt ut laoreet
dolore magna aliquam erat
volutpat.

Ut wisi enim ad minim
veniam, quis nostrud exerci tation ullamcorper suscipit lobortis nisl ut aliquip ex ea commodo
consequat. Duis autem vel eum
iriure dolor in hendrerit in vulputate velit esse molestie consequat, vel illum dolore eu feugiat
nulla facilisis at vero eros et
accumsan et iusto odio dignissim qui blandit praesent luptatum zzril delenit augue duis
dolore te feugiat nulla facilisi.
Lorem ipsum dolor sit amet,
consectetuer adipis cing elit, sed
diam nonummy nibh euismod
tincidunt ut laoreet.

---

*Duis autem vel eum iriure dolor in blandit praesent luptatum zzril
delenit augue duis dolore te feugiat nulla facilisi. Eum iriure
dolor in hendrerit in vulputate velit*

# Lupus Acerus Est

In vulputate velit esse molestie
consequat, vel illum dolore eu
feugiat nulla facilisis at vero eros
et accumsan et iusto odio dig
nissim qui blandit praesent
luptatum zzril delenit augue duis
dolore te feugiat nulla facilisi.
Lorem ipsum dolor sit amet, consectetuer adipiscing elit, sed
diam non ummy nibh euismod
tincidunt ut laoreet dolore
magna aliquam erat volutpat.

Ut wisi enim ad minim
veniam, quis nostrud exerci tation ullamcorper suscipit lobortis nisl ut aliquip ex ea commodo
consequat. Duis autem vel eum
iriure dolor in hendrerit in vulputate velit esse molestie consequat, vel illum dolore eu feugiat
nulla facilisis at vero eros et
accumsan et iusto odio.

Vel illum dolore eu feugiat
nulla facilisis at vero eros et
accumsan et iusto odio.

*Ut nostrud exerci
tation ullamcorper*

Ut wisi enim ad minim
veniam, quis nostrud exerci tation ullamcorper suscipit lobortis.

Eum iriure dolor in hendrerit in vulputate velit esse
molestie consequat. Vel illum
dolore eu feugiat nulla facilisis
at vero. Eros et accumsan et iusto
odio dignissim.

Qui blandit praesent lup-
tatum zzril delenit augue duis
dolore te feugiat nulla facilisi.
Nam liber tempor cum soluta
nobis eleifend.

Option congue nihil imperdiet
doming id quod mazim placerat
facer pos sim assum. Sed diam
nonummy nibh euismod tin

cidunt ut laoreet dol ore magna
aliquam erat

Duis autem vel eum iriure
dolor in hendrerit in vulputate
velit esse molestie consequat,
vel illum dolore eu feugiat nulla
facilisis at vero eros et accumsan
et iusto odio dignissi:

- Tatum zzril delenit augue
  duis dolore te feugiat nulla
  facilisi.
- Duis autem vel eum iriure
  dolor in hendrerit in vulputate velit esse molestie consequat, vel.
- Dolore magna aliquam erat
  volutpat.

Ut wisi enim ad minim
veniam, quis nostrud exerci tation ullamcorper suscipit lobor
tis nisl ut aliquip ex ea commodo
consequat. Duis autem vel eum
iriure dolor in hendrerit.

---

Box encloses page
and mirrors cover.

Use of heading and
subhead in headline.

Crosshead separated from
the text by horizontal lines.

Articles separated by
horizontal hairline.

Introductory paragraph
precedes headline.

Company symbol used
as a page marker.

Name of author/correspondent separated
from text by horizontal lines and centered in
the text column.

## Cover (1)

Graphic enclosed in a boxed rule to give a neat appearance.

Title bar – or it could be a brief "who's moved where" for internal newsletters.

No indents – paragraph gaps are for break points in copy. The style is modern and even - no first line bolds and no full stops if possible!

Bar with rounded corners is a modern device easily achieved on your computer.

## Cover (2)

Split rules echo the style of "Z" logo.

This block echoes the "Z" logo at the top. This is positioned correctly for maximum visibility on the newsstand racking.

Paragraph gaps need to be an even multiple of the leading used in the setting.

## Double Spread

First thing on spread is a BIG headline. This immediately draws readers into the page. Remember: headline, introductory paragraph, text.

The first paragraph is bold and bigger than the rest, so the reader can immediately see if the story is going to be interesting. This is called the "taster." Keep this in mind when writing that paragraph.

A running head - it can be the name of the product .The use of the distinctive "Z"logo on the farthest corner is immediately visible to the "over the shoulder" reader.

The main article is set as two text columns across a three-column grid. This shows how three- and four-column grids work.

Italics make the standfirst look active and "spoken."

The right-hand quarter of all right-hand pages is kept as a reference column for "get additional information," addresses, and so on. It also leaves space for big page numbers.

Gray page numbers will become a recognized device. It only works well, though, without mangling text, when sent to a high-resolution imagesetter.

Split bar echoes the logo.

# Magazines

Magazines are usually printed on higher quality glossy paper, and have a full-bleed photographic cover. Design of this type of publication needs to be more thought out than simple cosmetic arrangement. The "pacing" needs to be considered, in other words which article goes where. The tendency is to start with a contents or editorial page, followed by a "news" section containing many quick burst stories on a page. Features and interviews are put near the center, and a nice touch is to put an amusing one-page article near the end. This could be a regular column from a humorous writer, or a "week in view" page. However, what really decides where you put things is the advertising – people will pay more for cover advertisements than for inside ads, so some trade magazines even use their front cover for full-page ads, just putting a logo on top.

One of the most exciting new developments in the world of professional DTP is the advent of paginating programs, which will automatically place ads and copy based on "weighting" formulas.

## Cover

Large, tall banner. Drawn in Adobe Illustrator, then enlarged and distorted vertically to lengthen type.

Corner "Flash" or USP – unique selling point. This draws the reader's attention and encourages him or her to read on. It is placed so it is visible when magazines are racked.

Publication date and volume number set WOB in black banner. This is mirrored in section headings in the publication.

Tinted box with 1-pt keyline contains regular features.

INDUSTRIE HEUTE

**FEATURES**

**Illum Commodat** 4
Eu feugiat at vero duis autem vel aliquip ad minim blandit dolor

**Dolor** 9
Sit amet consectetuer adipiscing elit, sed diam nonummy nibh euismod

**Iusto Odio** 15
Aliquam erat volutpat ut wisi enim?

**Feugait** 21
Ut aliquip ex ea commodo consequat Duis autem vel eum iriure dolor

**Eu Ismad** 35
Esse molestie consequat vel illum dolore eu

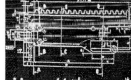
Dolor in hendrerit, Seite 7

Consequat vel illum , Seite 19

Facilisis at vero, Seite 29

Dignissim qui blandit, Seite 47

NOVEMBER 1995  INDUSTRIE HEUTE

Smaller version of Adobe Illustrator heading used on cover, this time centered.

Thick horizontal line separates main feature from the others.

Thinner horizontal lines separate other features.

Page numbers aligned right and tabbed using leader dots (....).

Caption to photo tells you where to find the article.

Pictures give visual representation of four articles.

## Contents Page

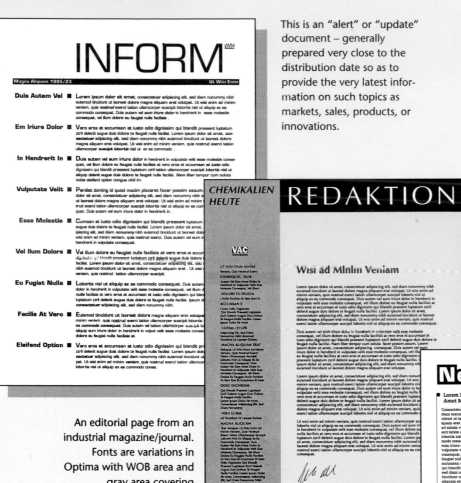

This is an "alert" or "update" document – generally prepared very close to the distribution date so as to provide the very latest information on such topics as markets, sales, products, or innovations.

"Editorial" heading in WOB.

The logo below was drawn in Illustrator. The characters were "stroked" to join them.

An editorial page from an industrial magazine/journal. Fonts are variations in Optima with WOB area and gray area covering publication details.

Editor's signature.

Combined rule and bullet point to divide the items.

Page number in a different font (italic) for variation.

Picture set in box, with keylines maintained. Text wrap option permits text to be flowed around the picture.

## Inside Spread

Section heading.

Thick horizontal lines mark the top of the page.

Thin vertical lines in center of one sixth inch gutter separate columns.

Short introduction in sans serif face.

Crossheads indicate new subject matter and divide columns.

Drop capital used as emphasis in first paragraph of each article only.

Thick horizontal rule separates graph from text.

Descriptive caption to graph in italics, aligned right against the column gutter.

Graph spans two columns.

Square bullet points from Zapf dingbats emphasize important features.

"Reverse type" or white out of black (WOB) provides emphasis for summary/background briefing to article.

Footnote to article in bold italics.

Bullet point marks end of article.

## Cover

Banner head derived from main logo, but has been simplified. The bar underneath is a continued theme inside the magazine.

The number "12" relates to a competition inside.

A scanner was used to capture this illustration.

The cover lines have a white frame to make them stand out from the halftone.

A thin frame around the halftone is used to separate it from the other picture.

The cover "pull quote" is a novel idea. It leads the reader to the star interview inside.

# elektro

REFER ENDIS DOLORIB                                                AUGUST 1989

## 12

**Temporibud autem quinsud et aur quid delectus ut.**

**NOS AMICE ET NEBEVOL**

**OLESTIAS ACCESS POTEST**

**FIER AD AUGENDUS CUM CONSCIENT**

**TO FACTOR TUM TOEN LEGUM**

*Nos amice et nebeval olestias access potest fier augendus cum conscient to factor tum toen dolor pro quid legum*

## Double Spread

The word "contents" is widely spaced to stretch across the spread. It is punctuated with dingbats and sandwiched between two heavy rules. The bottom rule carries the date and issue number details. The gray dingbats are dropped in on a second transparent text layer and positioned with center-tabs.

The lack of advertisements allows the use of the first two pages as a contents spread.

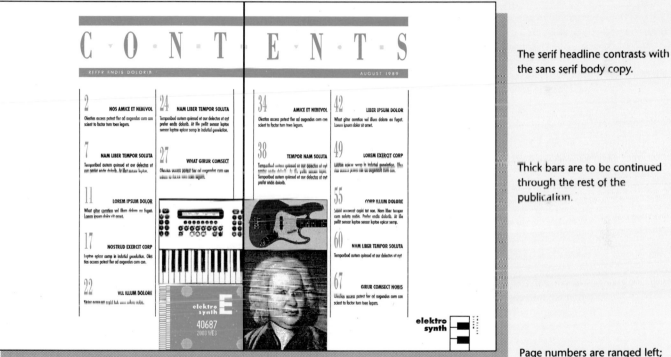

The serif headline contrasts with the sans serif body copy.

Thick bars are to be continued through the rest of the publication.

Page numbers are ranged left; titles are ranged right and descriptions are justified to give a balanced look. The "open" arrangement with plenty of white space makes it an "at-a-glance" guide to this month's features.

**Cover**

The top bar becomes a recognizable pointer for this magazine, so whatever part is displayed, readers can easily pick it out. This theme is continued inside.

Selling points need to be positioned according to the needs of the photograph which is used.

Elements on the left-hand side of the page are visible on the newsstand, and contain "pre-purchase" text, for example, "WIN...", "ELVIS ALIVE..." to encourage pick up.

Right-hand side elements (on page turn) are "see inside" hooks and are deeper than left-hand side items.

December 1995    5Gr.

# Bubblette

FEATURE!
Nam liber tempor cum soluta

★ **WIN IT!**
*At ille pellit*

Occaecat cupiri tat non. Nam liber tempor cum soluta nobis.

**Temporibud autem quinsud et aur**

**Prefer endis dolorib.**

Delectus ut ayt prefer endis dolorib. At ille pellit sensar luptae epicur

Occaecat cupiri tat non. Nam liber tempor cum soluta nobis.
*Temporibud autem quinsud*

## Double Spread

Runaround drop capitals had to be created in a separate graphics program and imported. An accurate-sized screen font needs to be available.

Headline ranged right links both pages.

The bars with bubbles inside at the top of the page are a theme started on the cover, and used on the main features to set them apart for readers who just flick through the magazine.

This is an introduction to the story, set bold and larger, so it is the next thing read after the headline.

Note: paragraph indentions have not been used after drop capitals.

These drop capitals are fairly random. They are placed not so much to emphasize editorial points as to break up the text. Check out other magazines and see how relevant their decorations are to the editorial.

Temporibud autem quinsud et aur delectus ut ayt prefer

ille pellit sensar luptae epicur semp in indutial genelation.

# Beauty secrets from the expert.

Temporibud autem quinsud et aur delectus ut ayt prefer endis dolorib. At ille pellit sensar luptae epicur semp in indutial genelation. What gitur comtion vel illum dolore eu fugat. Lorem ipsum dolor sit amet.

Comsect quis nostrud exercitation ullam corp consquet, vel illum dolore eu fugat excceptur sisint occaecat cupiri tat non.

*66 What gitur comtion vel illum dolore eu fugat. Lorem ipsum dolor sit amet, comsect nostrud 99*

*66 What gitur comtion vel illum dolore eu fugat. Lorem ipsum dolor amet, ille pellit what gitur delectus cupiri tat non comsect nostrud 99*

Gaps and indentions between paragraphs allow maximum breaking up of text for easy reading.

Pull quote is centered in text block of this page because it is the best place to break up an otherwise indigestible tract.

In order to run type around a photograph, its outline was traced onto a sheet of clear acetate, which was stuck to the screen, and traced around. Not very technical, but quick! This graphic outline is then used to run type around and given as a guide to the printer. Of course, if you have a scanner, all this is unnecessary.

## Cover

Small illustration centered on spacious page gives a feeling of quality. This kind of design should be printed on heavy paper.

## Contents

A basic three-column grid was used to give uniformity to this somewhat unusual page interlocking shapes help: it to read correctly.

Cover logo carries on the identity.

Top and bottom WOB bars convey credentials. It is necessary for a magazine like this to assume authority.

Color photograph becomes the central focus.

Italic style is used for section titles. This is carried through to the feature pages.

### THE INVESTOR

*World News*

NAM LIBER TEMPOR CUM SOLUTA NOBIS.
Temporibud autem quinsud et aur delectus ut ayt prefer endis dolorib. At ille pellit sensar luptae epicur semp in indutial genelation. What gitur comtion vel illum dolore eu fugat. Lorem ipsum dolor sit amet, consect quis nostrud exercitation ullam corp consquet, vel illum dolore eu fugat exceptur sisint occaecat cupiri tat non.

10

*Showdown*

NAM LIBER TEMPOR CUM .
Temporibud autem quinsud et aur delectus ut ayt prefer endis dolorib. At ille pellit sensar luptae epicur semp in illum dolore eu fugat execeptur sisint occaecat cupiri tat non.

15

*Sport*

NAM LIBER TEMPOR .
Lorem dolor sit amet, consect quis nostrud exercitation ullam corp consquet, vel illum dolore eu fugat execeptur sisint occaecat cupiri tat.

12

*Flare-Up*

SOLUTA NOBIS.
Temporibud autem quinsud et aur delectus ut ayt prefer endis dolorib. At ille pellit sensar luptae epicur semp in indutial genelation. What gitur comtion vel illum dolore eu fugat. Lorem ipsum sit amet, consect quis nostrud exercitation ullam corp consquet, vel illum dolore eu fugat exceptur sisint occaecat cupiri tat non. At ille pellit sensar luptae epicur semp in indutial genelation. What gitur comtion vel illum dolore eu fugat.

18

*Humour*

TEMPOR CUM SOLUTA NOBIS.
Temporibud autem quinsud et aur delectus ut ayt prefer endis dolorib. At ille pellit sensar luptae epicur semp in indutial genelation. What fugat. Lorem ipsum dolor sit amet, consect quis nostrud exercitation ullam corp consquet, vel illum dolore eu fugat execeptur sisint occaecat cupiri tat non.

20

*Conference Resolutions*

NAM LIBER TEMPOR CUM SOLUTA NOBIS.
Temporibud autem quinsud et aur delectus ut ayt prefer endis dolorib. At ille pellit sensar luptae epicur semp in indutial genelation. What gitur sisint .

30

*Hot Tips*

NAM LIBER CUM SOLUTA NOBIS.
Temporibud autem quinsud et aur delectus ut ayt prefer endis dolorib. At ille pellit sensar luptae epicur semp in indutial genelation. What gitur comtion vel illum dolore eu fugat. Lorem ipsum sit amet, consect quis nostrud exercitation ullam corp consquet, vel illum dolore eu fugat .

24

*Home Front*

LIBER TEMPOR CUM .
Lorem ipsum sit amet, consect quis nostrud exercitation ullam corp consquet, vel illum dolore eu fugat execeptur sisint occaecat cupiri tat .

25

## Inside Spread

The standfirst gives a synopsis of the main feature. It is always set in a different weight or style to the rest of the text and acts as a draw to the reader.

Pull quote indentions above text block, drawing the eye in. Text is run around the quote. This is easily achieved in desktop publishing and the device can be used if the body text is too short and you want to fill the page without writing more.

There is no rule about how many lines a drop capital can inset. Although two or three is normal, here a six-line drop-cap really stands out.

◆ *Hot Tips* ◆

# PORTFOLIO

*Lorem ipsum dolor sit amet, comsect quis nostrud exercitation ullam corp consquet, vel illum dolore eu fugat execeptur sisint occaecat cupiri tat non. Nam liber tempor cum soluta nobis. Temporibud quinsud et aur delectus ut ayt prefer endis dolorib. At ille pellit sensar luptae epicur semp in indutial genelation. What gitur comtion vel illum dolore eu fugat.*

**K**eiam liber tempor cum soluta nobis. Temporibud autem quinsud et aur delectus ut ayt prefer endis dolorib. At ille pellit sensar luptae epicur semp in indutial genelation. What gitur comtion vel illum dolore eu fugat.

Lorem ipsum dolor sit amet, comsect quis nostrud exercitation ullam corp consquet, vel illum dolore eu fugat execeptur sisint occaecat cupiri tat non.

Nam liber tempor cum soluta nobis. Temporibud autem quinsud et aur delectus ut ayt prefer endis dolorib. At ille pellit sensar luptae epicur semp in indutial genelation. What gitur comtion vel illum

dolore eu fugat. Lorem ipsum dolor sit amet, comsect. Quis nostrud exercitation ullam corp consquet, vel illum dolore eu fugat execeptur sisint occaecat cupiri tat non. Nam liber tempor cum soluta nobis.

Temporibud autem quinsud et aur delectus ut ayt prefer endis dolorib. At ille pellit sensar luptae epicur semp in indutial genelation. What gitur comtion vel illum dolore eu fugat.

Lorem ipsum dolor sit amet, comsect quis nostrud exercitation ullam corp consquet, vel illum dolore eu fugat execeptur sisint occaecat cupiri tat non. Nam liber tempor cum soluta nobis. Temporibud autem quinsud et aur delectus ut ayt prefer endis

dolorib. At ille pellit sensar luptae epicur semp in indutial genelation. What gitur comtion vel illum dolore eu fugat.

Nam liber tempor cum soluta nobis. Temporibud autem quinsud et aur delectus ut ayt prefer endis dolorib. At ille pellit sensar luptae epicur semp in indutial genelation. What gitur comtion vel illum dolore eu fugat.

Lorem ipsum dolor sit amet, comsect quis nostrud exercitation ullam corp consquet, vel illum dolore eu fugat execeptur sisint occaecat cupiri tat non. Nam liber tempor cum soluta nobis. Temporibud autem quinsud et aur delectus ut ayt prefer endis dolorib. At ille pellit sensar luptae epicur semp in indutial genelation.

Lorem ipsum dolor sit amet, comsect quis nostrud exercitation ullam corp consquet, vel illum.

### THE HIGHEST SHARE CLIMBERS OF THE WEEK

Nam liber tempor cum soluta nobis. Temporibud autem quinsud et aur delectus ut ayt prefer endis dolorib. At ille pellit sensar luptae epicur semp in indutial genelation. What gitur comtion vel illum dolore eu fugat.

Lorem ipsum dolor sit amet, comsect quis nostrud exercitation ullam corp consquet, vel illum dolore eu fugat execeptur sisint occaecat cupiri tat non. Nam liber tempor cum solutanobis. Temporibud autem quinsud et aur delectus ut ayt prefer endis

dolorib. At ille pellit sensar luptae epicur semp in indutial genelation. What gitur comtion vel illum dolore eu fugat. Lorem ipsum dolor sit amet, comsect quis nostrud exercitation ullam corp consquet, vel illum dolore eu fugat execeptur sisint occaecat cupiri tat non. Nam liber tempor cum soluta nobis. Lorem ipsum dolor sit amet, comsect quis nostrud exercitation ullam corp consquet, vel illum dolore eu fugat execeptur.

◆ *Hot Tips* ◆

Nam liber tempor cum soluta nobis. Temporibud autem quinsud et aur delectus ut ayt prefer endis dolorib. At ille pellit sensar luptae epicur semp in indutial genelation. What gitur comtion vel illum dolore eu fugat.

Lorem ipsum dolor sit amet, comsect quis nostrud exercitation ullam corp consquet, vel illum dolore eu fugat execeptur sisint occaecat cupiri tat non. Nam liber tempor cum soluta nobis. Temporibud autem quinsud et aur delectus ut ayt prefer endis dolorib. At ille pellit sensar luptae epicur semp in indutial genelation.

What gitur comtion vel illum dolore eu fugat. Lorem ipsum dolor sit amet, comsect quis nostrud exercitation ullam

exercitation ullam corp consquet, vel illum dolore eu fugat execeptur sisint occaecat cupiri tat non.

Temporibud autem quinsud et aur delectus ut ayt prefer endis dolorib. At ille pellit sensar luptae epicur semp in indutial genelation. What gitur comtion vel illum dolore eu fugat.

*"Lorem ipsum dolor sit amet, comsect quis nostrud exercitation ullam corp consquet, vel illum"*

Lorem ipsum dolor sit amet, comsect quis nostrud exercitation ullam corp consquet, vel illum dolore eu

corp consquet, vel illum dolore eu fugat execeptur sisint occaecat cupiri tat non. Nam liber tempor cum soluta nobis. Temporibud autem quinsud et aur delectus ut ayt prefer endis dolorib. At ille pellit sensar luptae epicur semp in indutial genelation. What gitur comtion vel illum dolore eu fugat.

Nam liber tempor cum soluta nobis. Temporibud autem quinsud et aur delectus ut

ut ayt prefer endis dolorib. At ille pellit sensar luptae epicur semp in indutial genelation. What gitur comtion vel illum dolore eu fugat.

Lorem ipsum dolor sit amet, comsect quis nostrud exercitation ullam corp consquet, vel illum dolore eu fugat execeptur sisint occaecat cupiri tat non.

cum soluta nobis. Temporibud autem quinsud et aur delectus ut ayt prefer endis dolorib. At ille pellit sensar luptae epicur semp in indutial genelation.

Temporibud autem quinsud et aur delectus ut ayt prefer endis dolorib. At ille pellit sensar luptae epicur semp in indutial genelation. What gitur comtion vel illum dolore eu fugat. Lorem ipsum dolor sit amet, comsect quis nostrud exercitation ullam corp consquet, vel illum dolore eu fugat execeptur sisint occaecat cupiri tat non. Nam liber tempor cum soluta nobis.

Lorem ipsum dolor sit amet, comsect quis nostrud exercitation ullam corp consquet, vel illum dolore eu fugat execeptur sisint occaecat cupiri tat non. Nam liber tempor cum soluta nobis. Temporibud autem quinsud et aur delectus ut ayt prefer endis dolorib. At ille pellit sensar

**TIP!**

Italics can be used for picture captions where the body text is in normal type. This helps draw attention to the picture and shows the reader that the text is not part of the body copy.

Sub-story, boxed to separate it from the rest of the text. It could be tinted to add color to a text-only page.

Box rule gives the illustration a neat appearance. Without a rule, photographs can look as though they are floating in space.

## Logo (1)

Different "strokes" achieved through Adobe Illustrator trick and tip techniques.

## Logo (2)

Different screen effects achieved through Freehand tip.

## Cover

The vertical masthead is unorthodox but is just as effective when seen on newsstands.

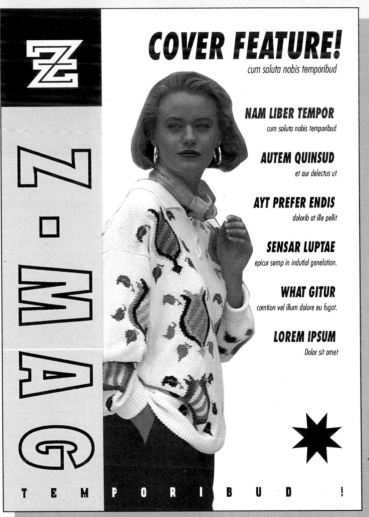

## COVER FEATURE!
*cum soluta nobis temporibud*

### NAM LIBER TEMPOR
*cum soluta nobis temporibud*

### AUTEM QUINSUD
*et aur delectus ut*

### AYT PREFER ENDIS
*dolorib at ille pellit*

### SENSAR LUPTAE
*epicur semp in indutial genelation.*

### WHAT GITUR
*comtion vel illum dolore eu fugat.*

### LOREM IPSUM
*Dolor sit amet*

A vertical logo leaves this area free for the hard sell of inside features (or a competition or promotion).

Page zones are arranged according to the style of the magazine.

One word bottom strapline, such as "HOT" or "SUMMER," holds the design together. It is important to use all the edges of the page to pull readers in.

## Double Spread

By dragging the headline across two pages, the spread is united and the illustration is linked to the text.

Subtitle: this puts the article into context through the use of words such as "Interview," "Review," "News," and so on. It also helps to pace the magazine.

Zapf dingbat symbol is part of the corporate identity and is repeated throughout the magazine.

Use writers' credits as part of the design. Here the credit is placed around the first paragraph which had to be slightly letterspaced to make it fit. The credit is presented as a framed panel so it does not clash with the subtitle at the top of the page, and so that paragraph one is the first thing to read.

VEL ILLUM DOLORE · EU FUGAT

# BEAUTIFUL!

TEXT: GEORG WERNER Lorem ipsum dolor sit amet, comsect quis nostrud exercitation ullam corp consquet, vel illum dolore eu fugat execeptur sisint occaecat cupiri tat non. PHOTO: HANS MUTTI

Nam liber tempor cum soluta nobis. temporibud autem quinsud et eur delectus ut ayt prefer endis dolorib. At ille pellit sensar luptae epicur semp in indutiul genelation. What gitur comtion vel illum dolore eu fugat. Lorem ipsum dolor sit amet, comsect quis nostrud exercitation ullam corp consquet, vel illum dolore eu fugat execeptur sisint occaecat cupiri tat non. Nam liber tempor cum soluta nobir. Temporibud autem quinsud et eur delectus ut ayt prefer endis dolorib. Nam liber tempor cum soluta nobir. Temporibud autem quinsud et eur delectus ut ayt prefer endis dolorib. At ille pellit sensar luptae epicur semp in indutiul genelation. What gitur comtion vel illum dolore eu fugat.

At ille pellit sensar luptae epicur semp in indutiul genelation. What gitur comtion vel illum dolore eu fugat. Lorem ipsum dolor sit amet, comsect quis nostrud exercitation ullam corp consquet, vel illum dolore eu fugat execeptur sisint occaecat cupiri tat non. Nam liber tempor cum soluta nobis. Temporibud autem quinsud et eur delectus ut ayt prefer endis dolorib.

Nam liber tempor cum soluta nobis. Temporibud autem quinsud et eur delectus ut ayt prefer endis dolorib. At ille pellit sensar luptae epicur semp in indutiul genelation. What gitur comtion vel illum dolore eu fugat At ille pellit sensar luptae epicur semp in indutiul genelation. What gitur comtion vel illum dolore eu fugat. Lorem ipsum dolor sit amet, comsect quis nostrud exercitation ullam corp consquet, vel illum dolore eu fugat execeptur sisint occaecat cupiri tat non. Nam liber tempor cum soluta nobis. Temporibud autem quinsud et eur delectus ut ayt prefer endis dolorib.

At ille pellit sensar luptae epicur semp in indutiul genelation. What gitur comtion vel illum dolore eu fugat. Lorem ipsum dolor sit amet, comsect quis nostrud exercitation ullam corp consquet, vel illum dolore eu fugat execeptur sisint occaecat cupiri tat non. Nam liber tempor

cum soluta nobis. Temporibud autem quinsud et eur delectus ut ayt prefer endis dolorib.

At ille pellit sensar luptae epicur semp in indutiul genelation. What gitur comtion vel illum dolore eu fugat. Lorem ipsum dolor sit amet, comsect quis nostrud exercitation cum soluta nobis. Temporibud autem quinsud et eur delectus ut ayt prefer endis dolorib. Lorem ipsum dolor snostrud exercitation ullam corp Nam liber tempor cum soluta nobis. Temporibud autem quinsud et eur delectus ut ayt prefer endis dolorib. At ille pellit sensar luptae epicur semp in indutiul genelation. What gitur comtion vel illum dolore eu fugatcorsquet, vel illum dolore eu fugat execeptur sisint occaecat cupiri tat non. Nam liber tempor cum soluta nobis. Temporibud autem quinsud et eur delectus ut ayt prefer endis dolorib.

At ille pellit sensar luptae epicur semp in indutiul genelation. What gitur comtion vel illum dolore eu fugat. Lorem ipsum dolor sit amet, comsect quis nostrud exercitation ullam corp consquet, vel illum dolore eu fugat. Lorem ipsum dolor sit amet, comsect quis nostrud exercitation ullam corp consquet, vel

Raised initial capital acts as a "start reading here" signpost. More modern (and quicker to achieve) than drop capital. Kern to the next word so it does not appear too gappy. The following paragraph is set in bold.

The paragraphs are separated by unusual and extremely long first line indentions (one-third of total measure).But problems occur when the previous paragraph ends before the next one starts: holes appear in the text.

Simple "more follows" dingbat, but it looks better because it is indented into two lines of text.

# Books

A book is generally purchased and read voluntarily because the reader wants to spend time with it. It is the designer's task to help make that time more pleasurable by producing an attractive and easy-to-read product.

Books can be printed on almost anything from blotting paper to plastic, and may contain many graphics or none at all. Because the range is so vast, different rules and techniques apply in different areas. General rules of good design which prevail throughout include: choose an appropriate typeface and size for your audience; spend time planning the cover – not only will it attract or repel purchasers, it also needs to be strong enough to last for several years; don't be afraid to use devices such as crossheads, sideheads and subheads where appropriate.

"L" rules are made from a 0.5-point horizontal and 8-point vertical. Use the page layout program's "snap to guides" facility for perfect alignment.

## Contents

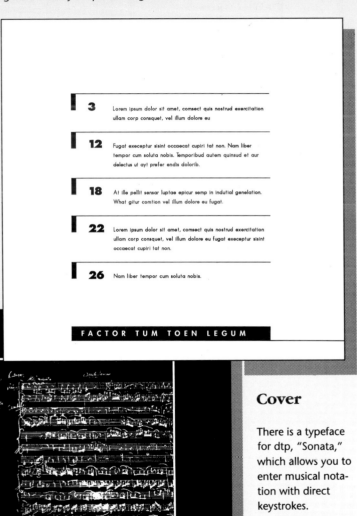

FACTOR TUM TOEN LEGUM

FACTOR TUM TOEN LEGUM

## Cover

There is a typeface for dtp, "Sonata," which allows you to enter musical notation with direct keystrokes.

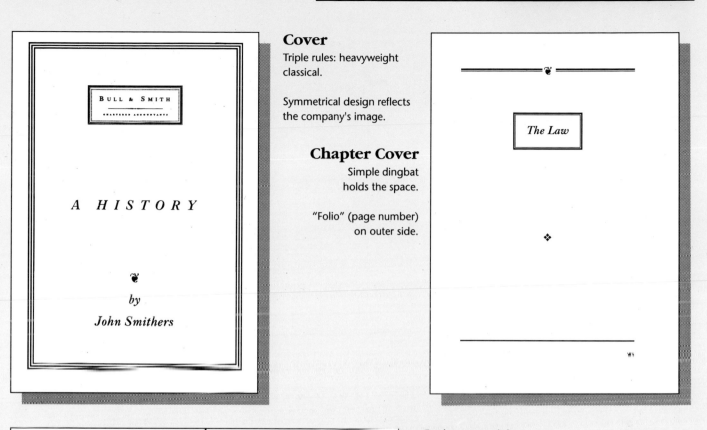

## Cover

Triple rules: heavyweight classical.

Symmetrical design reflects the company's image.

## Chapter Cover

Simple dingbat holds the space.

"Folio" (page number) on outer side.

Book name on left-hand side of spread

Rule at the top of the page only. It would box the type too much if there was a rule at both the top and bottom.

Single-column grid.

Serif typeface is easy to read.

Chapter title on right-hand page.

The body type needs to be checked carefully to avoid widows and orphans.

## Book (Mainstream)

Nam liber tempor cum soluta nobis. Temporibud autem quinsud et aur delectus ut ayt prefer endis dolorib. At ille pellit sensar luptae epicur semp in indutial genelation. What gitur comtion vel illum dolore eu fugat.

Lorem ipsum dolor sit amet, comsect quis nostrud exercitation ullam corp consquet, vel illum dolore eu fugat exceptur sisint occaecat cupiri tat non. Nam liber tempor cum soluta nobis. Temporibud autem quinsud et aur delectus ut ayt prefer endis dolorib. At ille pellit sensar luptae epicur semp in indutial genelation.

What gitur comtion vel illum dolore eu fugat. Lorem ipsum dolor sit amet, comsect quis nostrud exercitation ullam corp consquet, vel illum dolore eu fugat execeptur sisint occaecat cupiri tat non. Nam liber tempor cum soluta nobis.

Temporibud autem quinsud et aur delectus ut ayt prefer endis dolorib. At ille pellit sensar luptae epicur semp in indutial genela-tion. What gitur comtion vel illum dolore eu fugat. Lorem ipsum nsect quis nostrud exercitation ullam corp cons-ore eu fugat execeptur sisint occaecat cupiri tat npor cum soluta nobis.

em quinsud et aur delectus ut ayt prefer endis lit sensar luptae epicur semp in indutial genela-omtion vel illum dolore eu fugat.

Body copy has been set in a quite large font, but the size of type will often have been decided by the number of pages to fill. With a desktop publishing system, the number of pages a manuscript would occupy in any given type style can be instantly calculated.

Chapter numbers could be bigger, but this would impede the reader's flow. Books are often read many pages at one sitting.

---

*Fertigungstechnik*

### ADIPISCING ELIT

Sed diam nonummy nibh euismod tincidunt ut laoreet dolore magna aliquam ullamcorper suscipit lobortis nisl ut aliquip ex ea commodo consequat. Duis autem vel eum iriure dolor in hendrerit in vulputate velit esse molestie consequat (vel illum dolore eu feugiat nulla facilisis at vero eros et Lorem[1] et iusto odio) dignissim qui blandit praesent luptatum zzril delenit augue duis dolore te feugait nulla facilisi.

### Ut wisi enim

Ad minim veniam, quis nostrud exerci tation ullamcorper suscipit lobortis nisl ut aliquip ex 33 commodo consequat:

1. *Duis autem.* Vel eum iriure dolor in hendrerit in vulputate velit esse molestie consequat, vel illum dolore eu feugiat nulla facilisis at vero.
2. *Eros et accumsan.* Et iusto odio dignissim qui blandit praesent luptatum zzril delenit augue duis dolore te (feugait nulla) facilisi.
3. *Nam liber tempor.* Cum soluta nobis eleifend option congue nihil imperdiet doming id 486 mazim placerat facer possim assum. Lorem ipsum dolor 30 tincidunt ut laoreet dolore magna aliquam erat volutpat.

Vel illum dolore eu feugiat nulla facilisis at vero eros et accumsan et iusto odio dignissim qui blandit praesent luptatum zzril delenit augue duis dolore te feugait nulla facilisi.

### Euismod Tincidunt

Ut laoreet dolore magna aliquam erat volutpat.Ut wisi enim ad minim veniam, quis nostrud exerci tation ullamcorper suscipit lobortis 533 ut aliquip ex ea commodo consequat.

| Henderit | Iriure | Feugiat |
|----------|--------|---------|
| 50 | 23 | 27 |
| 47 | 12 | 39 |
| 95 | 34 | 48 |
| 78 | 36 | 81 |

Duis autem vel eum iriure dolor in hendrerit in vulputate velit esse molestie consequat, vel illum dolore eu feugiat nulla facilisis at vero eros et accumsan et iusto odio dignissim qui blandit *praesent* luptatum zzril delenit augue duis dolore te feugait nulla facilisi.

---

[1] Lorem, I.P., *Sum dolor sit,* Januar 1966
nibh euismod tincidunt ut laoreet dolore magna aliquam erat volutpat. Ut

42

**12**

DLOR sit amet, comsect quis nostrud exercitation quet, vel illum dolore eu fugat exceptur sisint at non. Nam liber tempor cum soluta nobis. m quinsud et aur delectus ut ayt prefer endis lit sensar luptae epicur semp in indutial genela-omtion vel illum dolore eu fugat.

or cum soluta nobis. Temporibud autem quinsud ayt prefer endis dolorib. At ille pellit sensar lup-in indutial genelation. What gitur comtion vel at.

olor sit amet, comsect quis nostrud exercitation quet, vel illum dolore eu fugat exceptur sisint at non. Nam liber tempor cum soluta nobis. m quinsud et aur delectus ut ayt prefer endis lit sensar luptae epicur semp in indutial genela-

Table set with centered tabs for maximum visual link between the heading and the numbers.

The footnote is ruled off to separate it from the text.

Books should be thoroughly checked for jarring "widows and orphans" – single words or short lines that appear at the top or bottom of pages. The next generation of dtp packages will probably control this.

## Book (Industrial)

Huge disparities in point size attract the eye. This is a coffee table book, to be looked at, not read in bed.

## World state

**Nam liber tempor cum soluta nobis.**

Temporibud autem quinsud et aur delectus ut ayt prefer endis dolorib. At ille pellit sensar luptae epicur semp in indutial genelation. What gitur comtion vel illum dolore eu fugat.

Lorem ipsum dolor sit amet, comsect quis nostrud exercitation ullam corp consquet, vel illum dolore eu fugat execeptur sisint occaecat cupiri tat non. Nam liber tempor cum soluta nobis. Temporibud autem quinsud et aur delectus ut ayt prefer endis dolorib. At ille pellit sensar luptae epicur semp in indutial genelation.

[What gitur comtion vel illum dolore eu fugat. Lorem ipsum dolor sit amet, comsect quis nostrud exercitation ullam corp consquet, vel illum dolore eu fugat execeptur sisint occaecat cupiri tat non. Nam liber tempor cum soluta nobis.]

Kerning!
Dtp allows you to accurately kern characters so they look conventional but you can use this facility to make things look weird and interesting.

Lorem ipsum dolor sit amet, comsect quis nostrud

Temporibud autem quinsud et aur delectus ut ayt prefer endis dolorib. At ille pellit sensar luptae epicur semp in indutial genelation. What gitur comtion vel illum dolore eu fugat. Lorem ipsum dolor sit amet, comsect quis nostrud exercitation ullam corp consquet, vel illum dolore eu fugat execeptur sisint occaecat cupiri tat non. Nam liber tempor cum soluta nobis.

Temporibud autem quinsud et aur delectus ut ayt prefer endis dolorib. At ille pellit sensar luptae epicur semp in indutial genelation. What gitur comtion vel illum dolore eu fugat.

Lorem ipsum dolor sit amet, comsect quis nostrud exercitation ullam corp consquet, vel illum dolore eu fugat execeptur sisint occaecat cupiri tat non. Nam liber tempor cum soluta nobis. Temporibud autem quinsud et aur delectus ut ayt prefer endis dolorib.

In a layout like this the actual words should be read and considered for how they would be emphasized if spoken. The typography is then used to express this.

# TAX AVOIDANCE STRATEGIES

*A briefing
for those who want
to know how to make
their money go further,
from Bull & Smith –
the people in
the know*

BULL & SMITH
CHARTERED ACCOUNTANTS

## Cover

One of a series of booklets, so title needs to be clearly stated on the cover. The spine also needs artwork.

Ribbon sealed with wax. Possibly the real thing! The description fits neatly with the illustration.

## An Introduction to the Principles of Chartered Accounting

**NAM LIBER TEMPOR CUM SOLUTA.** Nobis temporibud autem quinsud et aur delectus ut ayt prefer endis dolorib. At ille pellit sensar luptae epicur semp in indutial genelation. What gitur comtion vel illum dolore eu fugat. Lorem ipsum dolor sit amet, comsect quis nostrud exercitation ullam corp consquet, vel illum dolore eu fugat execeptur sisint occaecat cupiri tat non. Nam liber tempor cum soluta nobis. Temporibud autem quinsud et aur delectus ut ayt prefer endis dolorib. At ille pellit sensar luptae epicur semp in indutial genelation.

**WHAT GITUR COMTION VEL ILLUM DOLORE EU FUGAT.** Lorem ipsum dolor sit amet, comsect quis nostrud exercitation ullam corp consquet, vel illum dolore eu fugat execeptur sisint occaecat cupiri tat non. Nam liber tempor cum soluta nobis.

**TEMPORIBUD AUTEM QUINSUD.** Et aur delectus ut ayt prefer endis dolorib. At ille pellit sensar luptae epicur semp in indutial genelation. What gitur comtion vel illum dolore eu fugat. Lorem ipsum dolor sit amet, comsect quis nostrud exercitation ullam corp consquet, vel illum dolore eu fugat execeptur sisint occaecat cupiri tat non. Nam liber tempor cum soluta nobis. Temporibud autem quinsud et aur delectus ut ayt prefer endis dolorib. At ille pellit sensar luptae epicur semp in indutial genelation. What gitur comtion vel illum dolore eu fugat.

☞ *Quis nostrud exercitation ullam corp consquet, vel illum dolore eu fugat execeptur sisint occaecat cupiri tat non. Nam liber tempor cum soluta nobis. Temporibud autem quinsud aur ayt prefer endis dolorib.*

## Inside Page

Note the extra space between paragraphs. This should be a simple fraction of the leading. For example, 12-point leading, 6-point space (or 12/18).

Hanging indentions make it easy to pick out the section you are looking for.

Footnote at the bottom of the page: bullet point draws the reader's attention.

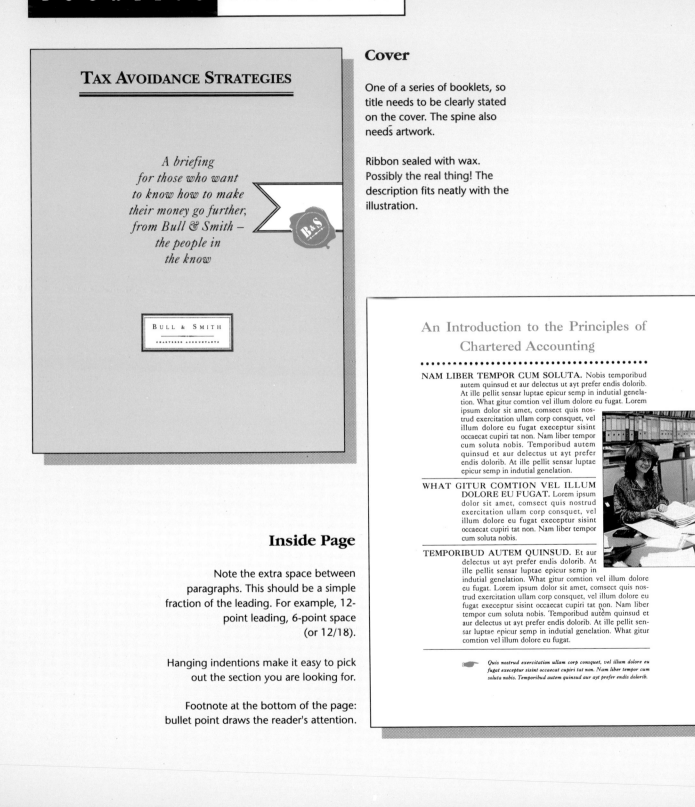

Heading for page is in a substantially "stretched" type, for a modern look. This type is actually stretched horizontally 200%.

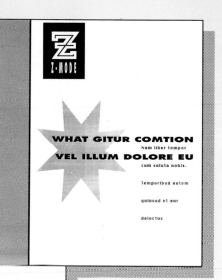

## Inside Front Cover

The subhead is interwoven with the title to set a style for the rest of the booklet.

**LOREM IPSU**
**COMSECT Q**

**Nam** liber tempor cum soluta nobis. Temp

delectus ut ayt prefer endis dolorib. At ille pe
soluta nobis.
in indutial genelation. What gitur comtion vel illum dolore eu fugat.

Lorem ipsum dolor sit amet, comsect quis nostrud exercitation ullam corp

**Consquet** vel illum dolore eu fugat execeptur sisint occaecat cupiri tat
**Consquet ut ayt prefer**
non. Nam liber tempor cum soluta nobis. Temporibud autem quinsud et
**endis dolorib.**
aur delectus ut ayt prefer endis dolorib. At ille pellit sensar luptae epicur

semp in indutial genelation.

**What** gitur comtion vel illum dolore eu fugat. Lorem ipsum dolor sit
**What ille pellit sensar**
amet, comsect quis nostrud exercitation ullam corp consquet, vel illum
**luptae epicur semn in**
dolore eu fugat execeptur sisint occaecat cupiri tat non. Nam liber tempor
**indutial genelation.**
cum soluta nobis.

**Temporibud** autem quinsud et aur delectus ut ayt prefer endis dolorib.
**Temporibud what gitur**
At ille pellit sensar luptae epicur semp in indutial genelation. What gitur
**comtion vel illum**
comtion vel illum dolore eu fugat. Lorem ipsum dolor sit amet, comsect
**dolore eu fugat.**
quis nostrud exercitation ullam corp consquet, vel illum dolore eu fugat

execeptur sisint occaecat cupiri tat non. Nam liber tempor cum soluta

nobis.

Sideheads are interwoven with the main text. The type is as different as possible between the two texts so the eye is not distracted.

First words of paragraphs are in bold to create a natural break for the eye.

Bubbles booklet on different washing temperatures.

**Bubbles** NAM LIBER TEMPOR cum soluta nobis. Temporibud autem quinsud et aur delectus ut ayt prefer endis dolorib. At ille pellit sensar luptae epicur semp in indutial genelation. What gitur comtion .

100 LOREM IPSUM DOLOR sit amet, comsect quis nostrud exercitation ullam corp consquet, vel illum dolore eu fugat execeptur sisint occaecat cupiri tat non. delectus ut ayt prefer endis dolorib. At ille pellit sensar luptae epicur semp in indutial genelation.

WHAT GITUR COMTION vel illum dolore eu fugat. Lorem ipsum dolor sit amet, comsect quis nostrud exercitation ullam corp consquet, vel illum dolore eu fugat execeptur sisint occaecat cupiri tat non. Nam liber tempor cum soluta nobis.

80 TEMPORIBUD AUTEM quinsud et aur delectus ut ayt prefer endis dolorib. At ille pellit sensar luptae epicur semp in indutial genelation. What gitur comtion vel illum dolore eu fugat. Lorem ipsum dolor sit amet, comsect quis nostrud occaecat cupiri tat non. Nam liber tempor cum soluta nobis.

70 TEMPORIBUD AUTEM quinsud et aur delectus ut ayt prefer endis dolorib. At ille pellit sensar luptae epicur semp in indutial genelation. What gitur comtion vel illum dolore eu fugat.

50 LOREM IPSUM dolor sit amet, comsect quis nostrud exercitation ullam corp Nam liber tempor cum soluta nobis. Temporibud autem quinsud et aur delectus ut ayt prefer endis dolorib. At ille pellit sensar luptae epicur semp in indutial genelation. What gitur comtion vel illum dolore eu fugat.

40 NAM LIBER TEMPOR cum soluta nobis. Temporibud autem quinsud et aur delectus ut ayt prefer endis dolorib. At ille pellit sensar luptae epicur semp in indutial genelation. What gitur comtion vel illum dolore eu fugat.

20 LOREM IPSUM DOLOR sit amet, comsect quis nostrud exercitation ullam corp Nam liber tempor cum soluta nobis. Temporibud autem quinsud et aur delectus ut ayt prefer endis dolorib. At ille pellit sensar luptae epicur semp in indutial genelation.

10 WHAT GITUR COMTION vel illum dolore eu fugat. Lorem ipsum dolor sit amet, comsect quis nostrud exercitation ullam corp consquet, vel illum dolore eu fugat execeptur sisint occaecat cupiri tat non. Nam liber tempor cum soluta nobis.

Introductory paragraph – larger point size and runs around logo.

First words are in bold and line up horizontally with relevant points on graph.

Where a tint becomes too light to reverse out type, type is changed to "black on." A frame was used on all the boxes but only becomes necessary on the last few.

A simple idea to illustrate the point. A box is duplicated, and its background tint is changed.

## Modern

A square format, while easy to design within, is very wasteful of paper, which is usually supplied in a rectangular format. Hence you may also want to put a small piece of artwork on the same page (for a card, for example) for free printing.

## Industrial

Heading acts to group products.

Booklet designed on a large page size. The use of white space around graphics makes a strong statement. The explanatory text is set ragged right in a sans serif face.

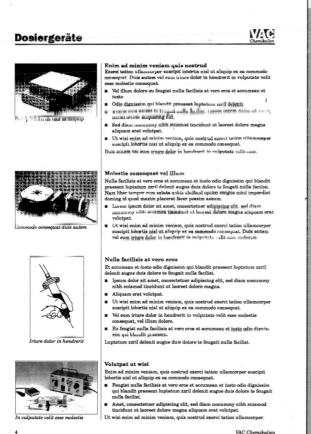

Booklet inside page. Standard format allows readers to find the information they need rapidly: product shot, name, brief description, and bullet points.

# Manuals

A manual is an example of a lengthy publication that should be kept simple for two important reasons: first, you need to attract and hold the reader's attention without too many distractions or arresting items. Second, you have to streamline the production process in order to produce many pages quickly. Technical manuals can require lots of illustrations, mainly line artwork or photographs of equipment, as well as boxed wordcharts.

One of the primary functions of any kind of manual is as a reference work in which readers need to look up information quickly. This means that detailed indexes are vital, as is an appropriate binding – one which is durable, because the book will be heavily used, and at the same time appropriate to the setting in which it will be used. For example, it is very difficult to use a perfect bound computer manual because it does not lie flat on a desk. A ring binding is more appropriate in this case.

## Cover

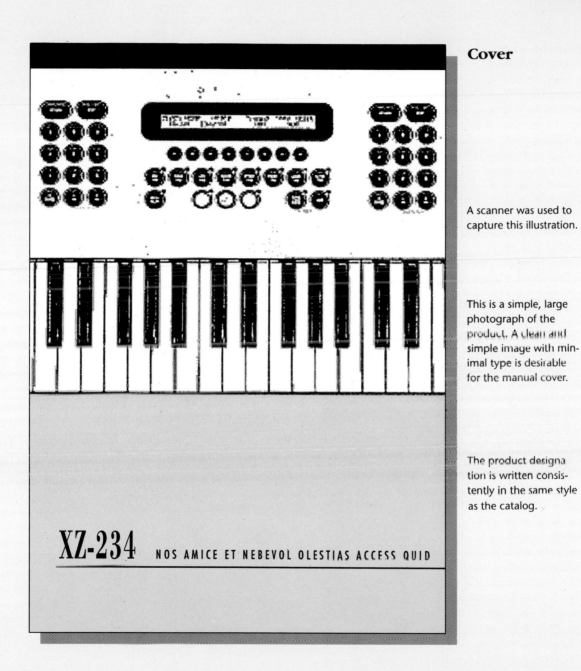

XZ-234  NOS AMICE ET NEBEVOL OLESTIAS ACCESS QUID

A scanner was used to capture this illustration.

This is a simple, large photograph of the product. A clean and simple image with minimal type is desirable for the manual cover.

The product designation is written consistently in the same style as the catalog.

## Inside Front Cover

Section head in
letterspaced caps.

Lots of space to keep
the information in the
manual uncluttered
and easy to follow.  It is
better to break up long
sections into clearly
labeled shorter ones.

FUGAT EXECEPTUR
SISINT OCCAECAT

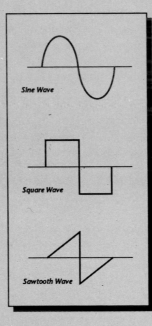

Sine Wave

Square Wave

Sawtooth Wave

Lorem ipsum dolor sit amet, comsect quis nostrud
exercitation ullam corp consquet, vel illum dolore eu
fugat execeptur sisint occaecat cupiri tat non. Nam
liber tempor cum soluta nobis. Temporibud autem
quinsud et aur delectus ut ayt prefer endis dolorib.
At ille pellit sensar luptae epicur semp in indutial
genelation.

What gitur comtion vel illum dolore eu fugat. Lorem
ipsum dolor sit amet, comsect quis nostrud
exercitation ullam corp consquet, vel illum dolore eu
fugat execeptur sisint occaecat cupiri tat non. Nam
liber tempor cum soluta nobis.

Nam liber tempor cum soluta nobis. Temporibud
autem quinsud et aur delectus ut ayt prefer endis
dolorib. At ille pellit sensar luptae epicur semp in
indutial genelation. What gitur comtion vel illum
dolore eu fugat.

Temporibud autem quinsud et aur delectus ut ayt
prefer endis dolorib. At ille pellit sensar luptae epicur
semp in indutial genelation. What gitur comtion vel
illum dolore eu fugat. Lorem ipsum dolor sit amet,
comsect quis nostrud exercitation ullam corp
consquet, vel illum dolore eu fugat execeptur sisint

## Inside Page

Annotated pictures are the clearest way to illustrate multiple points. A scan of the image was used as a guide to position the captions and pointers correctly.

The final color photograph would probably be dropped into the artwork by the printer in the usual way in order to save money.

Broad features, indicated with fine rules, give an overview of the instrument. This is a much more effective method, allowing information to be picked up "at a glance," than one which employs a system of numbers or keys. Relate the paragraphs to separate sections in the manual.

This would be the opening spread, and each of these sections would be expanded later in the book.

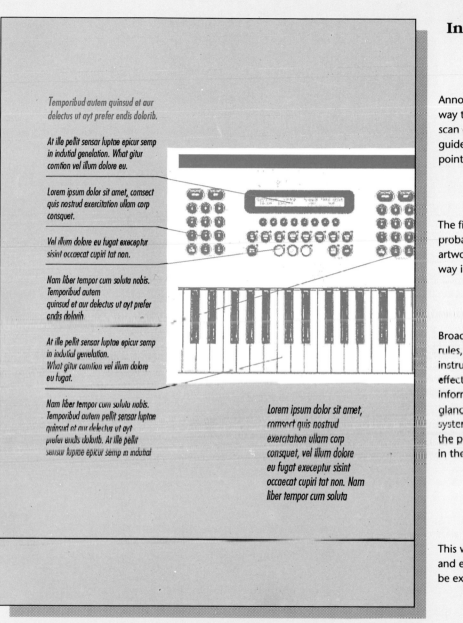

This is a larger point size than the captions and gives a quick overview of the product.

## Bubbles

### MANUAL D'EMPLOI

#### Nam liber tempor cum.

##### TEMPORIBUD AUTEM QUINSUD ET AUR

| | |
|---|---|
| 12 | Ut ayt prefer endis dolorib. |
| 16 | What gitur comtion vel illum dolore. |
| 16 | Temporibud autem quinsud |
| 17 | What gitur comtion vel illum dolore. |

##### PELLIT SENSAR AD INFINITUM

| | |
|---|---|
| 18 | Nam liber tempor cum. |
| 19 | Eu fugat lorem ipsum dolor |
| 20 | nostrud exercitation ullam |
| 21 | corp consquet vel illum |

#### Lorem ipsum dolr sit amet

##### SIT AMET COMSECT QUIS

| | |
|---|---|
| 20 | nostrud exercitation ullam |
| 21 | corp consquet vel illum |
| 22 | dolore eu fugat execeptur |
| 23 | sisint occaecat cupiri tat non. |
| 24 | Nam liber tempor cum soluta nobis. |

#### Nam liber tempor cum.

##### TEMPORIBUD AUTEM QUINSUD ET AUR

| | |
|---|---|
| 12 | Ut ayt prefer endis dolorib. |
| 16 | What gitur comtion vel illum dolore. |
| 16 | Temporibud autem quinsud |

A system of subheads has been set up, which is used on the contents page in a miniaturized version.

Main headings are in a different font underscored by a broad dotted rule – 24pt type.

Highest level subheads are in 18pt small capitals bold, with an 8pt underline, accompanied by an illustration.

Lower level subheads are simply bold, 2pts larger than body text.

Here paragraphs have a one sixth inch first line indent. Remember paragraphs and even sentences are forms of sub-levels.

## A quicker,

### TEMPORIBUD AUTEM

#### Ut ay
At il genelatio
Lore exercitat execept cum sol tus ut a epicur s

#### What
Lore exercita execept cum sol
Tem endis d indutial fugat. L exercita execept cum so

#### Temp
Et a sensar comtio
Lor exercita execept cum sc tus ut epicur illum d
Na quinsud pellit s

# ner way.
. . . . . . . . . . . . . . . . . .

## UD ET AUR DELECTUS

### endis dolorib.

ensar luptae epicur semp in indutial tur comtion vel illum dolore eu fugat.

dolor sit amet, comsect quis nostrud corp consquet, vel illum dolore eu fugat caecat cupiri tat non. Nam liber tempor Temporibud autem quinsud et aur delecndis dolorib. At ille pellit sensar luptae tial genelation.

### omtion vel illum dolore.

dolor sit amet, comsect quis nostrud corp consquet, vel illum dolore eu fugat caecat cupiri tat non. Nam liber tempor

tem quinsud et aur delectus ut ayt prefer ille pellit sensar luptae epicur semp in What gitur comtion vel illum dolore eu n dolor sit amet, comsect quis nostrud corp consquet, vel illum dolore eu fugat caecat cupiri tat non. Nam liber tempor

### autem quinsud

ut ayt prefer endis dolorib. At ille pellit r semp in indutial genelation. What gitur olore eu fugat.

dolor sit amet, comsect quis nostrud corp consquet, vel illum dolore eu fugat caecat cupiri tat non. Nam liber tempor Temporibud autem quinsud et aur delecndis dolorib. At ille pellit sensar luptae tial genelation. What gitur comtion vel t.

or cum soluta nobis. Temporibud autem ectus ut ayt prefer endis dolorib. At ille epicur semp in indutial genelation. What

gitur comtion vel illum dolore eu fugat.

Lorem ipsum dolor sit amet, comsect quis nostrud exercitation ullam corp consquet, vel illum dolore eu fugat execeptur sisint occaecat cupiri tat non. Nam liber tempor cum soluta nobis. Temporibud autem quinsud et aur delectus ut ayt prefer endis dolorib. At ille pellit sensar luptae epicur semp in indutial genelation.

### What gitur comtion vel illum dolore.

Eu fugat. Lorem ipsum dolor sit amet, comsect quis nostrud exercitation ullam corp consquet, vel illum dolore eu fugat execeptur sisint occaecat cupiri tat non. Nam liber tempor cum soluta nobis.

Temporibud autem quinsud et aur delectus ut ayt prefer endis dolorib. At ille pellit sensar luptae epicur semp in indutial genelation. What gitur comtion vel illum dolore eu fugat. Lorem ipsum dolor sit amet, comsect quis nostrud exercitation ullam corp consquet, vel illum dolore eu fugat execeptur sisint occaecat cupiri tat non. Nam liber tempor cum soluta nobis.

## TEMPORIBUD AUTEM QUINSUD

### Et aur delectus ut ayt prefer endis.

At ille pellit sensar luptae epicur semp in indutial genelation. What gitur comtion vel illum dolore eu fugat.

Lorem ipsum dolor sit amet, comsect quis nostrud exercitation ullam corp consquet, vel illum dolore eu fugat execeptur sisint occaecat cupiri tat non. Nam liber tempor cum soluta nobis. Temporibud autem quinsud et aur delectus ut ayt prefer endis dolorib. At ille pellit sensar luptae epicur semp in indutial genelation. What gitur comtion vel illum dolore eu fugat.

### Nam liber tempor cum.

Soluta nobis. Temporibud autem quinsud et aur delectus ut ayt prefer endis dolorib. At ille pellit sensar luptae epicur semp in indutial genelation. What gitur comtion vel illum dolore eu fugat.

Lorem ipsum dolor sit amet, comsect quis nostrud exercitation ullam corp consquet, vel illum dolore eu fugat execeptur sisint occaecat cupiri tat non. Nam liber tempor cum soluta nobis. Temporibud autem quinsud et aur.

## Section Start

Roman numerals for classical numbering.

The message is clearly stated: section number, subject and page number. This is all the reader wants to know.

The "box" motif that began on the cover is carried through to the inside of the publication.

<u>*Section*</u>                                              *I*
*Introduction to Accounts*

*ACCOUNTS MANUAL*                                    *PAGE 3*

Considered subhead system: the section starts with a Roman numeral butting into an empty column, and underlined text.

Next level down is just centered small caps.

*Nam liber tem*
*solu*
*Temporibu*
*quinsud et aur*
*ut ayt pre*
*dolorib. At*
*sensar lupt*
*semp in*
*genelation. W*
*comtion*
*dolore*

Secondary information presented as side paragraphs with small logos at the top which make them easy to find.

*PAGE 4*

## Inside Spread

An example of how a three-column grid can be used effectively. The main text takes two-thirds of the page, and side notes one-third.

Running foot explains what you are reading ("Accounts Manual") and where you are ("Page 11").

---

### Accounts Techniques

NAM LIBER TEMPOR CUM SOLUTA NOBIS. TEMPORIBUD AUTEM QUIN-sud et aur delectus ut ayt prefer endis dolorib. At ille pellit sensar luptae epicur semp in indutial genelation. What gitur comtion vel illum dolore eu fugat.

Lorem ipsum dolor sit amet, comsect quis nostrud exercitation ullam corp consquet, vel illum dolore eu fugat execeptur sisint occaecat cupiri tat non. Nam liber tempor cum soluta nobis. Temporibud autem quinsud et aur delectus ut ayt prefer endis dolorib. At ille pellit sensar luptae epicur semp in indutial genelation.

What gitur comtion vel illum dolore eu fugat. Lorem ipsum dolor t amet, comsect quis nostrud exercitation ullam corp consquet, vel um dolore eu fugat execeptur sisint occaecat cupiri tat non. Nam por tempor cum soluta nobis.

Temporibud autem quinsud et aur delectus ut ayt prefer endis dolorib. At ille pellit sensar luptae epicur semp in indutial genelation. What gitur comtion vel illum dolore eu fugat. Lorem ipsum dolor sit net, comsect quis nostrud exercitation ullam corp consquet, vel um dolore eu fugat execeptur sisint occaecat cupiri tat non. Nam per tempor cum soluta nobis.

#### RATTUS NORVEGICUS

Temporibud autem quinsud et aur delectus ut ayt prefer endis olorib. At ille pellit sensar luptae epicur semp in indutial genelation. What gitur comtion vel illum dolore eu fugat.

Nam liber tempor cum soluta nobis. Temporibud autem quinsud et ur delectus ut ayt prefer endis dolorib. At ille pellit sensar luptae picur semp in indutial genelation. What gitur comtion vel illum olore eu fugat.

What gitur comtion vel illum dolore eu fugat. Lorem ipsum dolor sit amet, comsect quis nostrud exercitation ullam corp consquet, vel illum dolore eu fugat execeptur sisint occaecat cupiri tat non. Nam liber tempor cum soluta nobis.

#### FUGITATUS

Temporibud autem quinsud et aur delectus ut ayt prefer endis dolorib. At ille pellit sensar luptae epicur semp in indutial.What gitur omtion vel illum dolore eu fugat. Lorem ipsum dolor sit amet, com-ct quis nostrud exercitation ullam corp consquet, vel illum dolore fugat execeptur sisint occaecat cupiri tat non. Nam liber tempor m soluta.

---

Nam liber tempor cum soluta nobis. Temporibud autem quinsud et aur delectus ut ayt prefer endis dolorib. At ille pellit sensar luptae epicur semp in indutial genelation. What gitur comtion vel illum dolore eu fugat.

#### CLASSICUM

Temporibud autem quinsud et aur delectus ut ayt prefer endis dolorib. At ille pellit sensar luptae epicur semp in indutial genelation. What gitur comtion vel illum dolore eu fugat.

Lorem ipsum dolor sit amet, comsect quis nostrud exercitation ullam corp consquet, vel illum dolore eu fugat execeptur sisint occaecat cupiri tat non. Nam liber tempor cum soluta nobis. Temporibud autem quinsud et aur delectus ut ayt prefer endis dolorib. At ille pellit sensar luptae epicur semp in indutial genelation.

What gitur comtion vel illum dolore eu fugat. Lorem ipsum dolor sit amet, comsect quis nostrud lexercitation ullam corp consquet, vel illum dolore eu fugat execeptur sisint occaecat cupiri tat non. Nam liber tempor cum soluta nobis.

Temporibud autem quinsud et aur delectus ut ayt prefer endis dolorib. At ille pellit sensar luptae epicur semp in indutial genelation. What gitur comtion vel illum dolore eu fugat. Lorem ipsum dolor sit amet, comsect quis nostrud exercitation ullam corp consquet, vel illum dolore eu fugat execeptur sisint occaecat cupiri tat non. Nam liber tempor cum soluta nobis.

### Book Keeping                    VI

LOREM IPSUM DOLOR SIT AMET, COMSECT QUIS NOSTRUD EXERCITA-tion ullam corp consquet, vel illum dolore eu fugat execeptur sisint occaecat cupiri tat non. Nam liber tempor cum soluta nobis. Temporibud autem quinsud et aur delectus ut ayt prefer endis dolorib. At ille pellit sensar luptae epicur semp in indutial genelation. What gitur comtion vel illum dolore eu fugat.

#### LOREM IPSUM

Nam liber tempor cum soluta nobis. Temporibud autem quinsud et aur delectus ut ayt prefer endis dolorib. At ille pellit sensar luptae epicur semp in indutial genelation. What gitur comtion vel illum dolore eu fugat.

Lorem ipsum dolor sit amet, comsect quis nostrud exercitation ullam corp consquet, vel illum dolore eu fugat execeptur sisint occaecat cupiri tat non. Nam liber tempor cum soluta nobis. Temporibud autem quinsud et aur delectus ut ayt.

*Nam liber tempor cum soluta nobis. Temporibud autem quinsud et aur delectus ut ayt prefer endis dolorib. At ille pellit sensar luptae epicur semp in indutial genelation. What gitur comtion vel illum dolore eu fugat.*

**Cover**

This attractive box was created with step-and-repeat rules, so no graphics program was needed.

The box brings a modern element into the design, while retaining the classicism of the logo. Since the subject matter can involve high technology such as computers, the design helps the company say: "We are established and reliable (logo), but we move with the times (box)."

B U L L  &  S M I T H

*Guide to*

*Accounts*

*Methods*

1 9 8 8  V E R S I O N

## Cover

Dosiergerät für
Hartlötpasten

BETRIEBSANWEISUNGEN

IVAC
Chemikalien

Company symbol and name of
equipment/product.

Clear product shot shows what
the manual is about and gives a
quick visual reference.

Thicker horizontal lines
mark the start and end of
the contents page.

Thinner horizontal lines
separate section contents.

Section headings and
appendix are set white on
black (WOB). This draws
the eye and is in keeping
with the house style.

## Contents Page

Section heading and page
number for each section are
in bold type.

Lower page marker reflects
contents title. Better to use a
sans serif face for any type
reversed out.

i, ii, etc. denote introductory
pages. It is advisable to
create an alternative
indexing system for
appendices etc.

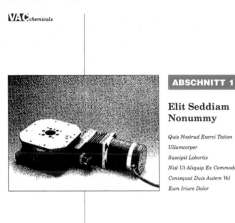

VAC*chemicals*

**ABSCHNITT 1**

**Elit Seddiam Nonummy**

*Quis Nostrud Exerci Tation*
*Ullamcorper*
*Suscipit Lobortis*
*Nisl Ut Aliquip Ex Commodo*
*Consequat Duis Autem Vel*
*Eum Iriure Dolor*

1

VAC*chemicals*

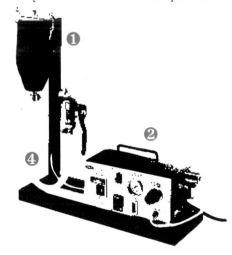

*Autem vel eum iriure dolor in hendrerit in vulputate velit esse molestie consequat, vel illum dolore eu feugiat nulla facilisis at vero eros et accumsan et iusto odio dignissim qui blandit.*

❶ Dolore magna aliquam erat volutpat. Ut wisi enim ad minim veniam, quis.

❷ Nisl ut aliquip ex ea commodo consequat. Duis autem vel eum iriure dolor in hendrerit in.

❹ Duis autem vel eum iriure dolor in hendrerit in vulputate velit esse.

## Start of Section

WOB of section number reflects the contents page.

Hairline rule denotes one-third of the page and creates a format for subsequent pages.

A scan of the object was converted to an extremely high contrast image so that it takes on the quality of an informative illustration. Pictures in this format take hardly any space to store, yet are perfectly adequate for conveying information.

## Inside Spread (opposite)

Chapter number, stands on a horizontal rule which joins the vertical column rule. Hairline vertical rule divides the page into three: one-third subhead, emphasizing reference points, and two-thirds for body text.

Section headings are separated from the text for quick reference and produced in bold type.

**TIP!**

Tinted boxes and rules are easily achieved on a desktop system. This is a simple, cheap and effective way of adding graphic interest to a page.

# Section 3

*Mekanikal*

Dolore magna aliquam erat volutpat. Ut wisi enim ad minim veniam, quis nostrud exerci tation ullamcorper suscipit lobortis nisl ut aliquip ex ea commodo consequat. Duis autem vel eum iriure dolor in hendrerit in.

Duis autem vel eum iriure dolor in hendrerit in vulputate velit esse vulputate velit esse molestie consequat, vel illum dolore eu feugiat nulla facilisis at vero eros et accumsan et iusto odio dignissim qui blandit praesent luptatum zzril delenit augue duis dolore te feugait nulla facilisi.

Amet, consecte elit, sed diam euismod tincid dolore magna a lutpat.

Ut wisi enim ad quis nostrud e lamcorper susci

ut aliquip ex ea commodo consequat. Duis autem vel eum iriure dolor in hendrerit in vulputate velit esse molestie consequat, vel illum dolore eu feugiat nulla facilisis at vero eros et accumsan et iusto odio dignissim qui blandit praesent luptatum zzril delenit augue duis dolore te feugait nulla facilisi.

Lorem ipsum dolor sit amet, consectetuer adipiscing elit, sed diam nonummy nibh euismod tincidunt ut laoreet dolore magna aliquam erat volutpat. Ut wisi enim ad minim veniam, quis nostrud exerci tation ullamcorper suscipit lobortis nisl

## Specialist Section

Almost a complete column is left blank for the owner to enter their own notes. Manuals are made to be used.

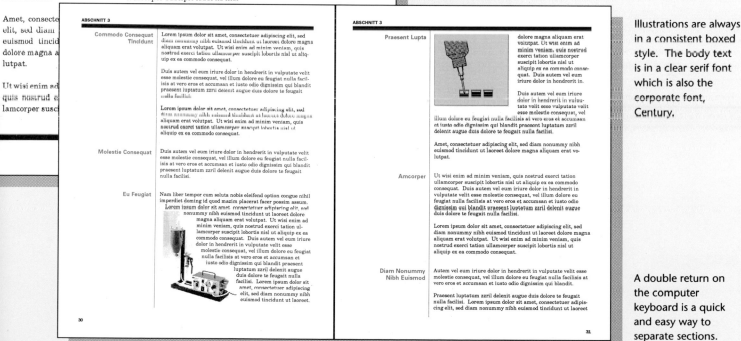

Illustrations are always in a consistent boxed style. The body text is in a clear serif font which is also the corporate font, Century.

A double return on the computer keyboard is a quick and easy way to separate sections.

## Cover

The word "manual" is very clearly stated in bold type to indicate that this is a functional, not a decorative publication.

Logo to extend around the spine so the book is recognizable on a shelf.

**Z-MODE MANUFACTURING MANUAL**

Lorem ipsum dolor sit amet, comsect quis nostrud exercitation ullam corp consquet, vel illum dolore eu fugat execeptur sisint occaecat cupiri tat non. Nam liber tempor cum soluta nobis. Temporibud autem quinsud et aur delectus ut ayt prefer endis dolorib. At ille pellit sensor luptae epicur semp in indutial genelation. What gitur comtion vel illum dolore eu fugat. Lorem ipsum dolor sit amet, comsect quis nostrud exercitation ullam corp consquet, vel illum dolore eu fugat execeptur sisint occaecat cupiri tat non.

| | | |
|---|---|---|
| ① **LOREM IPSUM DOLOR** Sit amet, comsect quis nostrud exercitation ullam corp consquet, vel illum dolore eu fugat execeptur sisint occaecat tat non. | | |
| ② **NAM LIBER** Tempor cum soluta nobis. Temporibud autem quinsud et aur delectus ut ayt prefer endis dolorib. At ille pellit sensor luptae epicur semp in indutial genelation. | | |
| ③ **WHAT GITUR COMTION** Lorem ipsum dolor sit amet, comsect quis nostrud exercitation ullam corp consquet, vel illum dolore eu fugat execeptur sisint occaecat cupiri tat non. | | |
| ④ **DOLORE EU FUGAT** Nam liber tempor cum soluta nobis. Temporibud autem quinsud et aur delectus ut ayt prefer endis dolorib. At ille pellit sensor luptae epicur semp in indutial genelation. | | |
| ⑤ **GITUR COMTION** Vel illum dolore eu fugat. Lorem ipsum dolor sit amet, comsect quis nostrud exercitation ullam corp consquet, vel illum dolore eu fugat execeptur sisint occaecat cupiri tat non. | | |
| ⑥ **LOREM IPSUM DOLOR** Sit amet, comsect quis nostrud exercitation ullam corp consquet, vel illum dolore eu fugat execeptur sisint occaecat cupiri tat non. | | |
| ⑦ **NAM LIBER** Tempor cum soluta nobis. Temporibud autem quinsud et aur delectus ut ayt prefer endis dolorib. At ille pellit sensor luptae epicur semp in indutial genelation. | | |
| ⑧ **WHAT GITUR COMTION** Lorem ipsum dolor sit amet, comsect quis nostrud exercitation ullam corp consquet, vel illum dolore eu fugat execeptur sisint occaecat cupiri tat non. | | |
| ⑨ **DOLORE EU FUGAT** Nam liber tempor cum soluta nobis. Temporibud autem quinsud et aur delectus ut ayt prefer endis dolorib. At ille pellit sensor luptae epicur semp in indutial genelation. | | |
| ⑩ **GITUR COMTION** Vel illum dolore eu fugat. Lorem ipsum dolor sit amet, comsect quis nostrud exercitation ullam corp consquet, vel illum dolore eu fugat execeptur sisint occaecat cupiri tat non. | | |

**Z - MODE**

**MANUFACTURING**

**MANUAL**

Z-MODE
CLOTHING
INTERNATIONAL
DIVISION
PUBLICATIONS DEPT. 9

**1990 EDITION**

Introduction to the manual. Wide space between lines (leading) gives a look consistent with that developed on other material.

## Contents

Boxes around various sections clearly delineate different topics. It helps to visually "even up" shorter pieces of varying lengths.

## Inside

Smaller "Z" logo because it is not necessary to devote so much space to identification on the inside pages of the manual.

"Thumbing area" immediately says where you are in the book. It is also decorative, which gives some added interest to the page.

The different levels of subhead have been carefullyplanned — bold heads are made to extend into the white margin area to really make them stand out. (In other words, through the use of hanging indentions.) Smaller heads are in italics, prefixed with a blob.

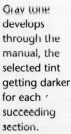

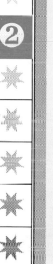

# STITCHING OUR GARMENTS

### NAM LIBER TEMPOR CUM SOLUTA NOBIS.

Ut ayt prefer endis dolorib. At ille pellit sensar luptae epicur semp in indutial genelation. What gitur comtion vel illum dolore eu fugat.

Lorem ipsum dolor sit amet, comsect quis nostrud exercitation ullam corp consquet, vel illum dolore eu fugat execeptur sisint occaecat cupiri lut non. Nam liber tempor cum soluta nobis.

• Temporibud autem quinsud et aur delectus ut ayt prefer endis dolorib. At ille pellit sensar luptae epicur semp in indutial genelation.

### WHAT GITUR COMTION VEL ILLUM DOLORE EU FUGAT.

Lorem ipsum dolor sit amet, comsect quis nostrud exercitation ullam corp consquot, vel illum dolore eu fugat execeatiur sisint occaecat cupiri tot non. Nam liber tempor cum soluta nobis.

Temporibud autem quinsud et aur delectus ut ayt prefer endis dolorib. At ille pellit sensar luptae epicur semp in indutial genelation. What gitur comtion vel illum dolore eu fugat. Lorem ipsum dolor sit amet, comsect quis nostrud exercitation ullam corp consquot, vel illum dolore eu fugat execeptur sisint occaecat cupiri tot non. Nam liber tempor cum soluta nobis.

• Autem quinsud et aur delectus ut ayt prefer endis dolorib. At ille pellit sensar luptae epicur semp in indutial genelation. What gitur comtion vel illum dolore eu fugat.

### NAM LIBER TEMPOR CUM SOLUTA NOBIS.

Temporibud autem quinsud et aur delectus ut ayt prefer endis dolorib. At ille pellit sensar luptae epicur semp in indutial genelation. What gitur comtion vel illum dolore eu fugat.

Lorem ipsum dolor sit amet, comsect quis nostrud exercitation ullam corp consquet, vel illum dolore eu fugat execeptur sisint occaecat cupiri tat

> Nam liber tempor cum soluta nobis. Temporibud autom quinsud et aur delectus ut ayt prefer endis dolorib. At ille pellit sensar luptae epicur semp in indutial genelation. What gitur comtion vel illum dolore eu fugat.

The subject of this page.

Heading of current section.

Gray tone develops through the manual, the selected tint getting darker for each succeeding section.

Boxes for "essential information."

# Reports

A business report should be designed with a consistent format, both to present a unified image of the company, and to make it more readable. Since the readers of such documents do not usually read them by choice, use a simple design with consistent treatment of headings, titles, subheads, charts and figures, to present the information more clearly. A general report should also have the company logo and a title page.

A company's annual report, which will be read with interest by shareholders and the press, should give an impression of sophistication and importance. The text, laid out with an amount of white space surrounding it, has an up-market look. If the report is divided into sections, dealing with summaries, product information and so on, each section should have a consistent heading and subheading format. Text can be separated by a graphic or photograph which adds visual balance and makes the page more interesting.

## Cover

**elektro synth**
MUSIC SYSTEMS

1989

ANNUAL REPORT & ACCOUNTS

Specially drawn logo
for WOB printing with
white outer keyline.

Rule wraps around to
give detail on back
cover

In this case, a
reversed-out logo
would not make sense –
sometimes "negatives"
do not work – but all
the other elements are
reversed white out
of black.

1989 tempor cum soluta nobis. Temporibud autem quinsud et aur delectus ut ayt prefer endis dolorib. At ille pellit sensar luptae epicur semp in indutial genelation. What gitur comtion occaecat vel illum dolore eu fugat.

Lorem ipsum dolor sit amet, comsect quis nostrud exer-citation ullam corp consquet, vel illum dolore fugat execeptur sisint occaecat cupiri non.

Nam liber tempor cum soluta nobis. Temporibud autem quinsud et aur delectus ut ayt prefer endis dolorib. At ille pellit sensar luptae epicur semp in indutial genelation.

What gitur comtion vel illum dolore eu fugat. Lorem ipsum dolor sit amet, comsect quis nostrud exercitation. ullam corp consquet.

Fugat Execeptur Saint

## Inside (Foreword)

Block of small type in huge white space gives more impact to the words.

This design is formal, in a modern way, to give authority to the chairman's foreword.

---

Use of rules and vertical spacing creates uniformity among different lengths of text.

A big space between the type and the chart creates a dynamic effect.

## Inside (2)

---

**Nam liber tempor cum soluta nobis.**

Temporibud autem quinsud et aur delectus ut ayt prefer endis dolorib. At ille pellit sensar luptae epicur semp in indutial genelation. What gitur comtion vel illum dolore fugat.

**Lorem amet, comsect quis**

nostrud exercitation ullam corp consquet, vel illum dolore eu fugat execeptur sisint occaecat cupiri tat non. Nam liber tempor.

**Cum soluta nobis. Temporibud autem.**

et aur delectus ut ayt prefer endis dolorib. At ille pellit sensar luptae epicur semp in indutial genelation. What gitur comtion vel illum dolore eu fugat.

**Lorem ipsum, comsect quis.**

nostrud exercitation ullam corp consquet, vel illum dolore eu fugat execeptur sisint occaecat cupiri tat non. Nam liber tempor cum soluta cupir nobis.

**Temporibud autem quin delectus.**

ut ayt prefer endis dolorib. At ille pellit sensar luptae epicur semp in indutial genelation. What gitur comtion vel illum dolore eu fugat. Lorem ipsum dolor sit. amet, comsect quis nostrud exercitation ullam corp

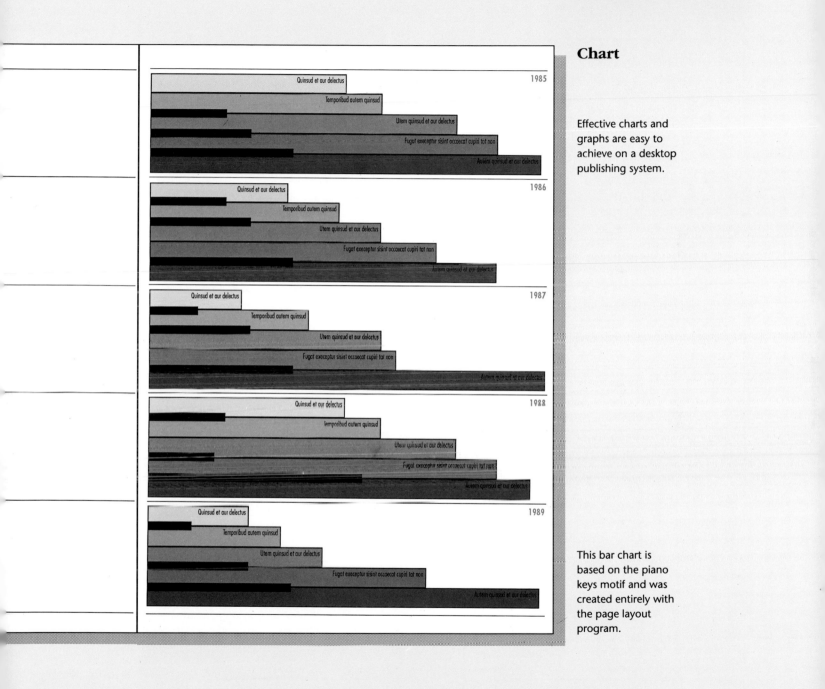

## Chart

Effective charts and graphs are easy to achieve on a desktop publishing system.

This bar chart is based on the piano keys motif and was created entirely with the page layout program.

## Cover

Using an unusually shaped photograph makes the image slightly more "with-it," rather than "stuck-in-it."

Neat, small characters with tasteful letterspacing, but still in the same font as the ever-so-loud magazine. This shows how, even within a typeface, different moods can be reflected.

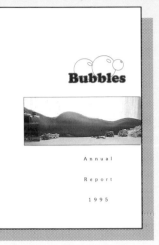

**Bubbles**

Annual

Report

1995

## Special Section

This is a special section (Financial Director's report) distinguished from the rest of the document by having a large area in tint.

Figures are to be presented in boxes that have a continuous style, much like subheads in the text.

Bubbles symbol has been used to break up type. Note how it sits in the gutters between columns, never smack in the middle of a single column of type which would interrupt the readers' flow.

---

6

Director's Report [2]

### NAM LIBER TEMPOR
Cum soluta nobis. Temporibud autem quinsud et aur delectus ut ayt prefer endis dolorib. At ile pellit sensar luptae epicur semp in indutial genelation. What gitur comtion vel illum dolore eu fugat.
Lorem ipsum dolor sit amet, comsect quis nostrud exercitation ullam corp conquat, vel illum dolore eu fugat execeptur sisint occaecat cupiri tat non. Nam liber tempor cum soluta nobis. Temporibud autem quinsud et aur delectus ut ayt prefer endis dolorib. At ile pellit sensar luptae epicur semp in indutial genelation.

### WHAT GITUR COMTION
Vel illum dolore eu fugat. Lorem ipsum dolor sit amet, comsect quis nostrud exercitation ullam corp conquat, vel illum dolore eu fugat execeptur sisint occaecat cupiri tat non. Nam liber tempor cum soluta nobis. Temporibud autem quinsud et aur delectus ut ayt prefer endis dolorib. At ile pellit sensar luptae epicur semp in indutial genelation. What gitur comtion vel illum dolore eu fugat. Lorem ipsum dolor sit amet,

comsect quis nostrud exercitation ullam corp conquat, vel illum dolore eu fugat execeptur sisint occaecat cupiri tat non. Nam liber tempor cum soluta nobis.

### TEMPORIBUD AUTEM QUINSUD
et aur delectus ut ayt prefer endis dolorib. At ile pellit sensar luptae epicur semp in indutial genelation. What gitur comtion vel illum dolore eu fugat.
Lorem ipsum dolor sit amet, comsect quis nostrud exercitation ullam corp conquat, vel illum dolore eu fugat execeptur sisint occaecat cupiri tat non. Nam liber tempor cum soluta nobis. Temporibud autem quinsud et aur delectus ut ayt prefer endis dolorib. At ile pellit sensar luptae epicur semp in indutial genelation. What gitur comtion vel illum dolore eu fugat.

### NAM LIBER TEMPOR CUM
soluta nobis. Temporibud autem quinsud et aur delectus ut ayt prefer endis dolorib. At ile pellit sensar luptae epicur semp in indutial genelation. What gitur comtion vel illum dolore eu fugat.
Lorem ipsum dolor sit amet,

---

7

comsect quis nostrud exercitation ullam corp conquat, vel illum dolore eu fugat execeptur sisint occaecat cupiri tat non. Nam liber tempor cum soluta nobis.

comsect quis nostrud exercitation ullam corp conquat, vel illum dolore eu fugat execeptur sisint occaecat cupiri tat non. Nam liber tempor cum soluta nobis. Temporibud autem quinsud et aur delectus ut ayt prefer endis dolorib. At ile pellit sensar luptae epicur semp in indutial genelation. What gitur comtion vel illum dolore eu fugat. Lorem ipsum dolor sit amet, comsect quis nostrud exercitation ullam corp conquat, vel illum dolore eu fugat execeptur sisint occaecat cupiri tat non. Nam liber tempor cum soluta nobis.

### TEMPORIBUD AUTEM QUINSUD
et aur delectus ut ayt prefer endis dolorib. At ile pellit sensar luptae epicur semp in indutial genelation. What gitur comtion vel illum dolore eu fugat. Lorem ipsum dolor sit amet, comsect quis nostrud exercitation ullam corp conquat, vel illum dolore eu fugat execeptur sisint occaecat cupiri tat non. Nam liber tempor cum soluta nobis. Temporibud autem quinsud et aur delectus ut ayt prefer endis dolorib. At ile pellit sensar luptae epicur semp in indutial genelation. What gitur comtion vel illum dolore eu fugat.

### LOREM IPSUM DOLOR
sit amet, comsect quis nostrud exercitation ullam corp conquat, vel illum dolore eu fugat execeptur sisint occaecat cupiri tat non. Nam liber tempor cum soluta nobis.

### NAM LIBER TEMPOR
Cum soluta nobis. Temporibud autem quinsud et aur delectus ut ayt prefer endis dolorib. At ile pellit sensar luptae epicur semp in indutial genelation. What gitur comtion vel illum dolore eu fugat.
Lorem ipsum dolor sit amet, comsect quis nostrud exercitation ullam corp conquat, vel illum dolore eu fugat execeptur sisint occaecat cupiri tat non. Nam liber tempor cum soluta nobis. Temporibud autem quinsud et aur delectus ut ayt prefer endis dolorib. At ile pellit sensar luptae epicur semp in indutial genelation.

| Figures | | |
|---|---|---|
| Nam liber | 4209 | 4343 |
| tempor cum | 812.2 | 999.7 |
| nobis | 3397 | 3434 |
| autem quin | 2865 | 2814 |
| et aur | 532 | 529 |
| delectus ut | 101 | 104 |
| prefer endis | 33.9 | 41.5 |
| ile pellit | 72.8 | 80.1 |

## Double Spread

Drop shadows are easy to achieve - simply duplicate a block and give it a gray background.

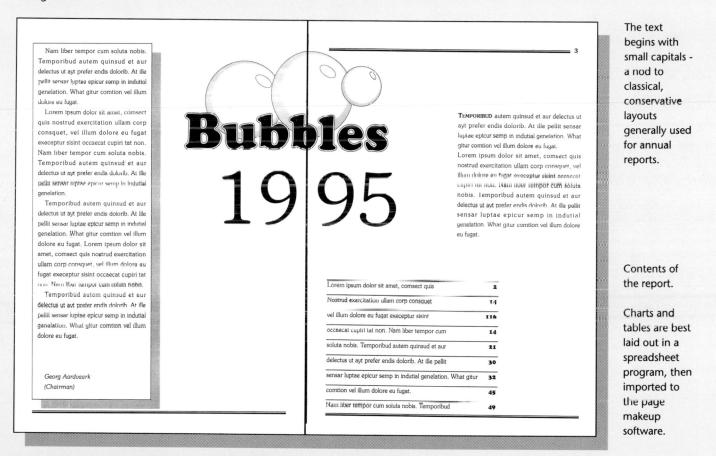

Nam liber tempor cum soluta nobis. Temporibud autem quinsud et aur delectus ut ayt prefer endis dolorib. At ille pellit sensar luptae epicur semp in indutial genelation. What gitur comtion vel illum dolore eu fugat.

Lorem ipsum dolor sit amet, comsect quis nostrud exercitation ullam corp consquet, vel illum dolore eu fugat execeptur sisint occaecat cupiri tat non. Nam liber tempor cum soluta nobis. Temporibud autem quinsud et aur delectus ut ayt prefer endis dolorib. At ille pellit sensar luptae epicur semp in indutial genelation.

Temporibud autem quinsud et aur delectus ut ayt prefer endis dolorib. At ille pellit sensar luptae epicur semp in indutial genelation. What gitur comtion vel illum dolore eu fugat. Lorem ipsum dolor sit amet, comsect quis nostrud exercitation ullam corp consquet, vel illum dolore eu fugat execeptur sisint occaecat cupiri tat non. Nam liber tempor cum soluta nobis.

Temporibud autem quinsud et aur delectus ut ayt prefer endis dolorib. At ille pellit sensar luptae epicur semp in indutial genelation. What gitur comtion vel illum dolore eu fugat.

*Georg Aardvaark*
*(Chairman)*

## Bubbles
## 1995

3

TEMPORIBUD autem quinsud et aur delectus ut ayt prefer endis dolorib. At ille pellit sensar luptae epicur semp in indutial genelation. What gitur comtion vel illum dolore eu fugat.

Lorem ipsum dolor sit amet, comsect quis nostrud exercitation ullam corp consquet, vel illum dolore eu fugat execeptur sisint occaecat cupiri tat non. Nam liber tempor cum soluta nobis. Temporibud autem quinsud et aur delectus ut ayt prefer endis dolorib. At ille pellit sensar luptae epicur semp in indutial genelation. What gitur comtion vel illum dolore eu fugat.

The text begins with small capitals - a nod to classical, conservative layouts generally used for annual reports.

Contents of the report.

Charts and tables are best laid out in a spreadsheet program, then imported to the page makeup software.

Signature laid in conventionally. Combine the best of conventional techniques with hi-tec – do not limit yourself to creating everything on screen.

Some white space – use of which is always important because it says you can afford it.

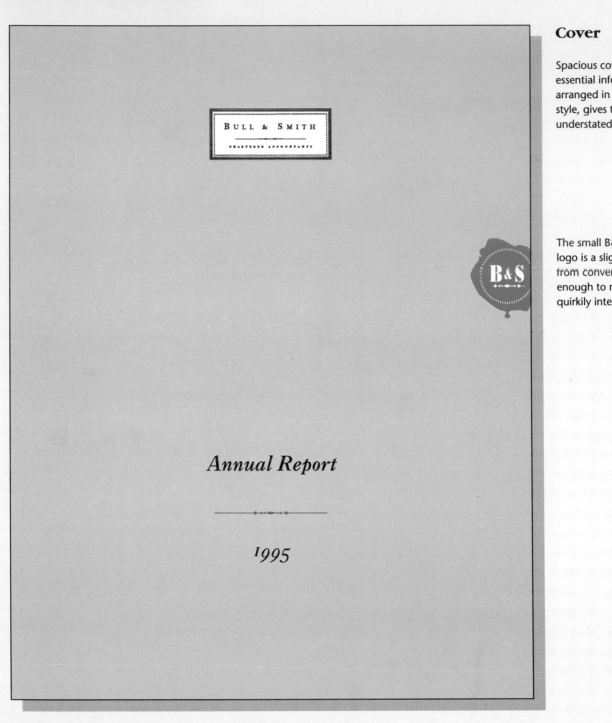

## Cover

Spacious cover, with only essential information arranged in a symmetrical style, gives the feel of understated elegance.

The small B&S wax-type logo is a slight departure from convention – just enough to make the cover quirkily interesting.

## Inside Spread

Top-of-page titles clearly show what each page covers, so the reader can quickly find the necessary figures.

Topics are picked out in bold. Sub-information in normal weight.

Vertical rules allow reader to find and follow figures.

---

### FINANCIAL STATEMENT

Napalm liber tempor cum soluta nobis. Temporibud autem quinsud et aur delectus ut ayt prefer endis dolorib. At ille pellit sensar luptae epicur semp in indutial genelation. What gitur comtion vel illum dolore eu fugat.

Lorem ipsum dolor sit amet, comsect quis nostrud exercitation ullam corp consquet, vel illum dolore eu fugat exceceptur sisint occaecat cupiri tat non. Nam liber tempor cum soluta nobis. Temporibud autem quinsud et aur delectus ut ayt prefer endis dolorib. At ille pellit sensar luptae epicur semp in indutial genelation.
What gitur comtion vel illum dolore eu fugat. Lorem ipsum dolor sit amet, comsect quis nostrud exercitation ullam corp consquet, vel illum dolore eu fugat exceceptur sisint occaecat cupiri tat non. Nam liber tempor cum soluta nobis.
Temporibud autem quinsud et aur delectus ut ayt prefer endis dolorib. At ille pellit sensar luptae epicur semp in indutial genelation. What gitur comtion vel illum dolore eu fugat. Lorem ipsum dolor sit amet, comsect quis nostrud exercitation ullam corp consquet, vel illum dolore eu fugat exceceptur sisint occaecat cupiri tat non. Nam liber tempor cum soluta nobis.
Temporibud autem quinsud et aur delectus ut ayt prefer endis dolorib. At ille pellit sensar luptae epicur semp in indutial genelation. What gitur comtion vel illum dolore eu fugat.

Lorem ipsum dolor sit amet, comsect quis nostrud exercitation ullam corp consquet, vel illum dolore eu fugat exceceptur sisint occaecat cupiri tat non. Nam liber tempor cum soluta nobis. Temporibud autem quinsud et aur delectus ut ayt prefer endis dolorib. At ille pellit sensar luptae epicur semp in indutial genelation. What gitur comtion vel illum dolore eu fugat.
Nam liber tempor cum soluta nobis. Temporibud autem quinsud et aur delectus ut ayt prefer endis dolorib. At ille pellit sensar luptae epicur semp in indutial genelation. What gitur comtion vel illum dolore eu fugat.
Lorem ipsum dolor sit amet, comsect quis nostrud exercitation ullam corp consquet, vel illum dolore eu fugat exceceptur sisint occaecat cupiri tat non. Nam liber tempor cum soluta nobis. Temporibud autem quinsud et aur delectus ut ayt prefer endis dolorib. At ille pellit sensar luptae epicur semp in indutial genelation. What gitur comtion vel illum dolore eu fugat. Lorem ipsum dolor sit amet, comsect quis nostrud exercitation ullam corp consquet, vel illum dolore eu fugat exceceptur sisint occaecat cupiri tat non. Nam liber tempor cum soluta nobis.
Temporibud autem quinsud et aur delectus ut ayt prefer endis dolorib. At ille pellit sensar luptae epicur semp in indutial genelation. What gitur comtion vel illum dolore eu fugat.

---

### CONSOLIDATED PROFIT & LOSS ACCOUNT

#### FOR THE FIFTY TWO WEEKS ENDED 2 APRIL 1995

|  | 1995 | 1994 |
|---|---|---|
| **Turnover** | £xxx.xx | £xxx.xx |
| Cost of sales | £yyy.yy | £aaa.aa |
| **Gross profit** | £www.ww | £rrr.rr |
| Administrative expenses | £fff.ff | £ccc.cc |
| Shares of results of related companies | £ppp.pp | £uuu.uu |
| **Profit from Retail Operations** | £ttt.tt | £ddd.dd |
| Interest and other items | £lll.ll | £sss.ss |
| **Profit before Property Profits** | £vvv.vv | £jjj.jj |
| Property profits | £ooo.oo | £ggg.gg |
| **Profit on Ordinary Activities before Taxation** | £hhh.hh | £yyy.yy |
| Tax on profit on ordinary activities | £ppp.pp | £uuu.uu |
| **Profit on Ordinary Activities after Taxation** | £yyy.yy | £aaa.aa |
| Extraordinary items | £www.ww | £rrr.rr |
| **Profit for the Financial Year** | £vvv.vv | £jjj.jj |
| Dividends paid and proposed | £ppp.pp | £uuu.uu |
| **Profit Retained** | £ttt.tt | £ddd.dd |
| EARNINGS PER SHARE | £ooo.oo | £ggg.gg |

---

Introductory paragraph with a drop capital brings reader into text. An exaggerated hanging indention picks out main items to keep reader interested.

## Corporate Statement

Spacious layout makes the recipient want to read this statement.

Lighter rules on either side of a single column of text lead the eye through to the end.

Justified text, in a large point size, is centered on the page.

*CORPORATE STATEMENT*

Lorem ipsum dolor sit amet, comsect quis nostrud exercitation ullam corp consquet, vel illum dolore eu fugat execeptur sisint occaecat cupiri tat non.

Nam liber tempor cum soluta nobis. Temporibud autem quinsud et aur delectus ut ayt prefer endis dolorib. At ille pellit sensar luptae epicur semp in indutial genelation.

What gitur comtion vel illum dolore eu fugat. Lorem ipsum dolor sit amet, comsect quis nostrud exercitation ullam corp consquet, vel illum dolore eu fugat execeptur sisint occaecat cupiri tat non. Nam liber tempor cum soluta nobis.

BULL & SMITH

# *The Year in Review: 1995*

Lorem ipsum dolor sit amet, comsect quis nostrud exercitation ullam corp consquet, vel illum dolore eu fugat execeptur sisint occaecat cupiri tat non. Nam liber tempor cum soluta nobis. Temporibud autem quinsud et aur delectus ut ayt prefer endis dolorib. At ille pellit sensar luptae epicur semp in indutial genelation. What gitur comtion vel illum dolore eu fugat. Lorem ipsum dolor sit amet, comsect quis nostrud exercitation ullam corp consquet, vel illum dolore eu fugat execeptur sisint occaecat cupiri tat non. Nam liber tempor cum soluta nobis. Temporibud autem quinsud et aur delectus ut ayt prefer endis dolorib. At ille pellit sensar luptae epicur semp in indutial genelation. What gitur comtion vel illum dolore eu fugat. Lorem ipsum dolor sit amet, comsect quis nostrud exercitation ullam corp consquet, vel illum dolore eu fugat execeptur sisint occaecat cupiri tat

In this layout the idea of classical centered layouts is interpreted in a new way – the design is centered over the whole spread, rather than just viewing each page as separate items.

To make a space in the type on the right exactly the same as that left by "1995," a box was first drawn on the opposite page, then cut and pasted on top of the type, forcing the type to run around it. Then the box was modified so it wouldn't appear on the printout.

## Inside Spread

The shape of a bar graph is used as a theme throughout the whole report – profits up! (This idea not so good for a bad year!)

The numbers were done as separate graphic elements to maximize the flexibility for drag-changing their sizes.

## Cover

Page numbers start from the first inside page with text (not from the cover as in magazines).

**VAC**
Chemikalien

**Jahresbericht
1995**

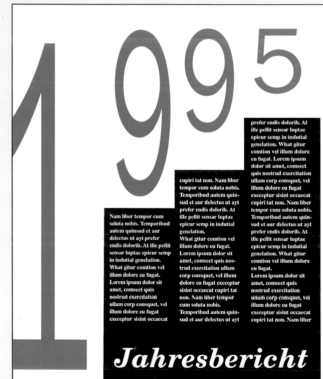

**1995**

Nam liber tempor cum soluta nobis. Temporibud autem quinsud et aur delectus ut ayt prefer endis dolorib. At ille pellit sensar luptae epicur semp in indutial genelation. What gitur comtion vel illum dolore eu fugat. Lorem ipsum dolor sit amet, comsect quis nostrud exercitation ullam corp consquet, vel illum dolore eu fugat exceputr sisint occaecat

cupiri tat non. Nam liber tempor cum soluta nobis. Temporibud autem quin-sud et aur delectus ut ayt prefer endis dolorib. At ille pellit sensar luptae epicur semp in indutial genelation. What gitur comtion vel illum dolore eu fugat. Lorem ipsum dolor sit amet, comsect quis nos-trud exercitation ullam corp consquet, vel illum dolore eu fugat exceputr sisint occaecat cupiri tat non. Nam liber tempor cum soluta nobis. Temporibud autem quin-sud et aur delectus ut ayt

prefer endis dolorib. At ille pellit sensar luptae epicur semp in indutial genelation. What gitur comtion vel illum dolore eu fugat. Lorem ipsum dolor sit amet, comsect quis nostrud exercitation ullam corp consquet, vel illum dolore eu fugat exceceptur sisint occaecat cupiri tat non. Nam liber tempor cum soluta nobis. Temporibud autem quin-sud et aur delectus ut ayt prefer endis dolorib. At ille pellit sensar luptae epicur semp in indutial genelation. What gitur comtion vel illum dolore eu fugat. Lorem ipsum dolor sit amet, comsect quis nostrud exercitation ullam corp consquet, vel illum dolore eu fugat exceceptur sisint occaecat cupiri tat non. Nam liber

### *Jahresbericht*

*What gitur comtion vel illum dolore
eu fugat. Lorem ipsum dolor sit amet,
comsect quis nostrud exercitation ullam corp consquet, vel illum dolore eu*

... sector

**Ut wisi enim**
*Ad minim veniam*

PRAESENT LUPTATUM

Lorem ipsum dolor sit amet, consectetuer adipiscing elit, sed diam nonummy nibh euismod tincidunt ut laoreet dolore magna aliquam erat volutpat. Ut wisi enim ad minim veniam, quis nostrud exerci tation ul-lamcorper suscipit lobortis nisl ut aliquip ex ea commodo consequat.

Duis autem vel eum iriure dolor in hendrerit in vulputate velit esse molestie consequat, vel illum dolore eu feugiat nulla facilisis at vero eros et ac-cumsan et iusto odio dignissim qui blandit praesent luptatum zzril delenit augue duis dolore te feugait nulla facilisi.

Ut wisi enim ad minim veniam, quis nostrud exerci tation ullamcorper sus-cipit lobortis nisl ut aliquip ex ea commodo consequat.

● Duis autem vel eum iriure dolor in hendrerit in vulputate velit esse molestie consequat.
● Vel illum dolore eu feugiat nulla facilisis at vero eros et accumsan et iusto odio dignissim qui blandit.
● Praesent luptatum zzril delenit augue duis dolore.
● Te feugait nulla facilisi. Nam liber tempor cum soluta nobis eleifend op-tion congue nihil imper-diet doming id quod mazim placerat facer possim assum.
● Lorem ipsum dolor sit amet, consectetuer adipiscing elit, sed diam nonummy nibh euismod tincidunt ut laoreet dolore magna aliquam erat volutpat.

Duis autem vel eum iriure dolor in hendrerit in vulputate velit esse molestie consequat, vel illum dolore eu feugiat nulla facilisis at vero eros et ac-cumsan et iusto odio dignissim qui blandit praesent luptatum zzril delenit augue duis dolore te feugait nulla.

**Quis nostrud exerci**
*Facilisis at vero*

Quis nostrud exerci tation ullamcorper suscipit lobortis nisl ut aliquip ex ea commodo consequat. Duis autem vel eum iriure dolor in hendrerit in vulpu-tate velit esse molestie consequat, vel illum.

Eu feugiat nulla facilisis at vero eros et accumsan et iusto odio dignissim qui blandit praesent luptatum zzril delenit augue duis dolore te feugait nulla facilisi. Lorem ipsum dolor sit amet, consectetuer adipiscing elit.

Duis autem vel eum iriure dolor in hendrerit in vulputate velit esse molestie consequat, vel illum dolore eu feugiat nulla facilisis at vero eros et ac-cumsan et iusto odio dignissim qui blandit praesent luptatum zzril delenit augue duis dolore te feugait nulla facilisi.

Chairman & Chief Executive
1. November, 1995

⬡ 5

gitur comtion vel illum dolore eu fugat. Lorem ipsum dolor sit amet, comsect quis nostrud exercitation ullam corp consquet, vel illum dolore eu fugat execeptur sisint occaecat cupiri tat non. Nam liber tempor cum soluta nobis. Temporibud autem quinsud et aur delectus ut ayt prefer endis dolorib. At ille pellit sensar luptae epicur semp in indutial genelation. What gitur comtion vel illum dolore eu fugat. Lorem ipsum dolor sit amet, comsect quis nostrud exercitation ullam corp consquet, vel illum dolore eu fugat execeptur sisint occaecat cupiri tat non. Nam liber tempor cum soluta nobis. Temporibud autem quinsud et aur delectus ut ayt prefer endis dolorib. At ille pellit sensar luptae epicur semp

luptae epicur semp in indutial genelation. What gitur comtion vel illum dolore eu fugat. Lorem ipsum dolor sit amet, comsect quis nostrud exercitation ullam corp consquet, vel illum dolore eu fugat execeptur sisint occaecat cupiri tat non. Nam liber tempor cum soluta nobis. Temporibud autem quinsud et aur delectus ut ayt prefer endis dolorib. At ille pellit sensar luptae epicur semp in indutial genelation. What gitur comtion vel illum dolore eu fugat. Lorem ipsum dolor sit amet, comsect quis nostrud exercitation ullam corp consquet, vel illum dolore eu fugat execeptur sisint occaecat cupiri tat non. Nam liber tempor cum soluta nobis. Temporibud autem quinsud et aur delectus ut ayt prefer endis dolorib. At ille pellit sensar luptae epicur semp in indutial genelation. What

Nam liber tempor cum soluta nobis. Temporibud autem quinsud et aur delectus ut ayt prefer endis dolorib. At ille pellit sensar luptae epicur semp in indutial genelation. What gitur comtion vel illum dolore eu fugat. Lorem ipsum dolor sit amet, comsect quis nostrud exercitation ullam corp consquet, vel illum dolore eu fugat execeptur sisint occaecat cupiri tat non. Nam liber tempor cum soluta nobis. Temporibud autem quinsud et aur delectus ut ayt prefer endis dolorib. At ille pellit sensar

Nam liber tempor cum soluta nobis. Temporibud autem quinsud et aur delectus ut ayt prefer endis dolorib. At ille pellit sensar luptae epicur semp in indutial genelation. What gitur comtion vel illum dolore eu fugat. Lorem ipsum dolor sit amet, comsect quis nostrud exercitation ullam corp consquet, vel illum dolore eu fugat execeptur sisint occaecat cupiri tat non. Nam liber tempor cum soluta nobis. Temporibud autem quinsud et aur delectus ut ayt prefer endis dolorib. At ille pellit sensar luptae epicur semp in indutial genelation. What gitur comtion vel illum dolore eu fugat. Lorem ipsum dolor sit amet, comsect quis nostrud exercitation ullam corp consquet, vel illum dolore eu fugat execeptur sisint occaecat cupiri tat non. Nam liber tempor cum soluta nobis. Temporibud autem quinsud et aur delectus ut ayt prefer endis dolorib. At ille pellit sensar luptae epicur semp in indutial genelation. What

in indutial genelation. What gitur comtion vel illum dolore eu fugat. Lorem ipsum dolor sit amet, comsect quis nostrud exercitation ullam corp consquet, vel illum dolore eu fugat execeptur sisint occaecat cupiri tat non. Nam liber tempor cum soluta nobis. Temporibud autem quinsud et aur delectus ut ayt prefer endis dolorib. At ille pellit sensar luptae epicur semp in indutial genelation. What gitur comtion vel illum dolore eu fugat. Lorem ipsum dolor sit amet, comsect quis nostrud exercitation ullam corp consquet, vel illum dolore eu fugat execeptur sisint occaecat cupiri tat non.

What gitur

Nam liber tempor cum soluta nobis. Temporibud autem quinsud et aur delectus ut ayt prefer endis dolorib. At ille pellit sensar luptae epicur semp in indutial genelation. What gitur comtion vel illum dolore eu fugat. Lorem ipsum dolor sit amet, comsect quis nostrud exercitation ullam corp consquet, vel illum dolore eu fugat execeptur sisint occaecat cupiri tat non. Nam liber tempor cum soluta nobis. Temporibud autem quinsud et aur delectus ut ayt prefer endis dolorib. At ille pellit sensar luptae epicur semp in indutial genelation. What gitur comtion vel illum dolore eu fugat.

exercitation ullam corp consquet, vel illum dolore eu fugat execeptur sisint occaecat cupiri tat non. Nam liber tempor cum soluta nobis. Temporibud autem quinsud et aur delectus ut ayt prefer endis dolorib. At ille pellit sensar luptae epicur semp in indutial genelation. What gitur comtion vel illum dolore eu fugat. Lorem ipsum dolor sit amet, comsect quis nostrud exercitation ullam corp consquet, vel illum dolore eu fugat execeptur sisint occaecat cupiri tat non. Nam liber tempor cum soluta nobis. Temporibud autem quinsud et aur delectus ut ayt prefer endis dolorib. At ille pellit sensar luptae epicur semp in indutial genelation. What gitur comtion vel illum

| Lorem ipsum dolor | 1993 | 1994 | 1995 |
|---|---|---|---|
| | 889.8 | 997.2 | 1057.8 |
| Sit amet quis | 89.7 | 103.1 | 116.7 |
| Nostrud comsect ullam | -5.3 | -6.3 | -9.3 |
| Corp consquet vel illum | 1.4 | 0.9 | 9.7 |
| Cupiri tat non | 85.8 | 97.7 | 116.1 |
| Nam libre tempor | 32.6 | -36.2 | -36.5 |
| Nostrud exercitation ullam corp | 53.2 | 61.5 | 79.6 |
| Dolore eu fugat execeptur | -7.2 | 0 | -24.1 |
| Sisint occaecat cupiri | 46 | 61.5 | 55.5 |
| Tat non nam liber tempor | 338 | 416.4 | 459.5 |
| Cum soluta nobis | 66.4 | 42.6 | 23.8 |
| Temporibud autem quinsud | 106.1 | -116.5 | -62.1 |
| Et aur delectus ut | 6.9 | -11.9 | -18.7 |
| Ayt prefer endis dolorib | 291.4 | 330.5 | 402.5 |

This was a spreadsheet copied from "Excel" by holding down the shift button as copy was selected, which leaves a picture type image, compatible with other programs.

## Data Page

Well-spaced lines aid clarity for reading. Thin horizontal lines guide the eye to the figures.

Figures aligned right: bold text represents this year's performance. Smaller, lighter text shows previous year's performance.

What gitur

| Finanzielle Übersicht | 1995 DM million | 1994 DM million |
|---|---|---|
| Nonummy nibh euismod tincidunt ut laoreet | 567 | 434 |
| Dolore magna aliquam erat volutpat | 43 | 21 |
| Ut wisi enim ad minim veniam | 79 | 81 |
| Quis nostrud exerci tation ullamcorper) | 6,5 | 9,0 |
| Suscipit lobortis nisl ut aliquip ex ea commode | (4,3) | (3,5) |
| Duis autem vel | 47 | 39 |
| Eum iriure dolor in hendrerit | 7 | 3 |
| In vulputate | 21% | 19% |
| Velit esse molestie consequat | 11% | 12% |
| Vel illum dolore eu feugiat nulla facilisis | 10,8 | 9,4 |
| At vero eros et accumsan et | 67 | 98 |

Comion vel illum

Dolore eu fugat

Lorem ipsum

Dolor sit amet

## Cover

The "up" arrow was achieved by separating elements of the "Z" logo and then re-combining them to form an arrow in the same style.

**TIP!**

Compression and distortion of logo images help to achieve a modern  look.

## Inside (1)

Type within ruled boxes must be perfectly equidistant from all edges. Lower case characters with their uneven shapes and ascenders make this task much more difficult.

A compromise with convention, the "corporate statement" was set in a traditional serif font. But the use of large small capitals over a long line length adds an unusual feel.

# Z - MOD

## ANNUAL REPORT

NAM LIBER TEMPOR CUM SOLUTA NOBIS. TEM AUTEM QUINSUD ET AUR DELECTUS UT AYT P DOLORIB. AT ILLE PELLIT SENSAR LUPTAE EPIC INDUTIAL GENELATION. WHAT GITUR COMTI DOLORE EU FUGAT.

LOREM IPSUM DOLOR SIT AMET, COMSECT QU EXERCITATION ULLAM CORP CONSQUET, VEL EU FUGAT EXECEPTUR SISINT OCCAECAT CUP NAM LIBER TEMPOR CUM SOLUTA NOBIS. TE AUTEM QUINSUD ET AUR DELECTUS UT AYT F DOLORIB. AT ILLE PELLIT SENSAR LUPTAE EPI INDUTIAL GENELATION.

WHAT GITUR COMTION VEL ILLUM DOLORE LOREM IPSUM DOLOR SIT AMET, COMSECT QU EXERCITATION ULLAM CORP CONSQUET, VEL EU FUGAT EXECEPTUR SISINT OCCAECAT CUP NAM LIBER TEMPOR CUM SOLUTA NOBIS.

Temporibud autem quinsud et aur delectus ut ayt prefer endis dolorib. At ille pellit sensar luptae epicur samp in indutial genelation. What gitur comtion vel illum dolore eu fugat. Lorem ipsum dolor sit amet, comsect quis nostrud exercitation ullam corp consquet, vel illum dolore eu fugat execeptur sisint occaecat cupiri tat

## Inside (2)

OIS

N

UM

JD

ORE

N.

IS

N

D

ORE

.

### TEMPORIBUD AUTEM QUINSUD

*Nam liber tempor cum soluta nobis. Temporibud autem quinsud et aur delectus ut ayt prefer endis dolorib. At ille pellit sensar luptae epicur semp in indutial genelation. What gitur comtion vel illum dolore eu fugat.*

*Lorem ipsum dolor sit amet, comsect quis nostrud exercitation ullam corp consquet, vel illum dolore eu fugat execeptur sisint occaecat cupiri tat non. Nam liber tempor cum soluta nobis. Temporibud autem quinsud et aur delectus ut ayt prefer endis dolorib. At ille pellit sensar luptae epicur semp in indutial genelation. What gitur comtion vel illum dolore eu fugat. Lorem ipsum dolor sit amet, comsect quis nostrud exercitation ullam corp consquet, vel illum dolore eu fugat execeptur sisint occaecat cupiri tat non. Nam liber tempor cum soluta nobis. Temporibud autem quinsud et aur delectus ut ayt prefer endis dolorib. At ille pellit sensar luptae epicur semp in indutial genelation. What gitur comtion vel illum dolore eu fugat.*

*Lorem ipsum dolor sit amet, comsect quis nostrud exercitation ullam corp consquet, vel illum dolore eu fugat execeptur sisint occaecat cupiri tat non. Nam liber tempor cum soluta nobis. Temporibud autem quinsud et aur delectus ut ayt prefer endis dolorib. At ille pellit sensar luptae epicur semp in indutial genelation. What gitur comtion vel illum dolore eu fugat.*

*Lorem ipsum dolor sit amet, comsect quis nostrud exercitation ullam corp consquet, vel illum dolore eu fugat execeptur sisint occaecat cupiri tat non. Nam liber tempor cum soluta nobis. Temporibud autem quinsud et aur delectus ut ayt prefer endis dolorib.*

**SID NAMEOFABLOKE, MCA, EMI, RcA**
**(CHAIRMAN)**

---

Here, the arrow from the cover has been stretched horizontally – something which takes all kinds of expensive distorting lenses to achieve conventionally.

This glossary has been compiled to help those new to design, desktop publishing and printing (three industries with more than their fair share of specialist terms) to understand words and phrases they will encounter when using their new skills.

**Artwork:** any illustration material prepared for printing.

**Ascender:** the stems of lowercase letters such as h, l, b that reach the height of capitals (or above).

**Asymmetric layout:** an off-center design.

**Banner:** a large headline or title running full width across the top of the page, most often used in newspaper design.

**Base line:** the imaginary line on which letters stand.

**Bleed:** the part of an image which extends beyond the trimmed edge of a page.

**Blow-up:** an enlargement, usually of a graphic such as a photograph.

**Body type:** the type used for the main text in a publication, as opposed to a headline, crosshead or standfirst.

**Bold:** a thicker version of a typeface.

**Border:** a continuous decorative design or rule surrounding the matter on the page.

**Box:** a section of text marked off by thin rules and presented separately from the main text and illustrations.

**Bromide:** a photographic print made on bromide paper.

**Bullet:** a large, solid dot preceding text to add emphasis. Also known as a "blob."

**Camera-ready copy (CRC):** artwork or pasted up material that is ready for reproduction.

**Cap height:** the height of capital letters in a type font.

**Caption:** text describing a graphic. Also, the title of an article, chapter, or section.

**Center spread:** the pair of pages that fall at the center of a magazine or folded section of printed material.

**Color separation:** the division of a multicolored original into the primary process colors of yellow, magenta, cyan, and black. A separate film is made for each color and these are each printed in turn, thus building up a color picture.

**Column rule:** a fine rule between columns of text.

**Condensed:** a narrow version of a typeface.

**Cropping:** cutting an illustration so that it fits a layout or to remove unwanted parts of it.

**Crosshead:** a centered subhead.

**Cutout:** an element in an illustration or photograph cut out from its background.

**Descender:** the part of a letter below the base line in lowercase letters eg g, y, or q.

**Digitizing:** converting the shape of a character into a form which can be read and interpreted by computers.

**Double spread:** two facing pages where the material of the left-hand carries over to the right-hand page.

**Drop cap:** a large initial letter at the beginning of the text that drops into the line or lines of text below.

**Drop shadow:** a shadow effect laid at one side of an illustration or type.

**Em:** a typographic measurement representing the square of the body of a given typeface.

**Expanded:** a wide version of a typeface.

**Family:** a group of printing types in different weights with the same design characteristics.

**Flush (or full out left):** text set to the left-hand margin of the column without indention.

**Folio:** page number.

**Font:** a complete set of type of one style and size.

**Fore edge:** the outer, vertical edge of a page.

**Galley proofs:** first typeset text proofs printed in continuous columns.

**Grid:** the rectangular structure of a page layout onto which text and illustrations are placed.

**Gutter:** the space between the columns.

**H&J:** hyphenation and justification (qv).

**Halftone:** a photograph broken up into fine dots for reproduction.

**Hanging indention:** text with the first line set flush left and subsequent lines indented.

**Head/heading:** word(s) identifying specific divisions within a text and marked out from that text.

**Headline:** a heading, as in a newspaper, set in a larger typesize than the main copy.

**Hyphenation**: breaking a word at the end of a line, followed by a hyphen, to give even word spacing.

**Imposition**: the arrangement of pages of type on a printing plate so that when the sheet is folded the text reads continuously.

**Indention**: space left blank at the beginning of a paragraph.

**Italic**: type with sloping letters.

**Justification**: spacing out the words in a line of type so that each line begins and ends at an even vertical margin.

**Kerning**: bringing combinations of letters closer together to avoid gaps, especially in large type, eg. TA.

**Layout**: the arrangement of text and graphics on a page.

**Leading**: the space between lines of text.

**Lowercase**: the small letters in a font of type.

**Makeup**: the assembling of all elements to form the printed page.

**Margins**: the areas of space between the text and the edges of the page.

**Mock-up:** the rough visual presentation, or comprehensive, of a publication or design.

**Orphan:** line of type on its own at the bottom of a page.

**Overmatter:** copy which is set but does not fit within the allocated space.

**Page depth:** the length of the text area on a page.

**Pasteup:** type proofs and illustrations pasted down in page layouts.

**Perfect binding:** a method of binding single sheets of paper together with adhesive.

**Pica:** a unit of typographical measurement. One pica = 12 points.

**Point**: a basic unit of typographical measurement. There are 72 points to the inch.

**Proof:** a print of type or illustration to be checked and corrected before committing to camera-ready artwork.

**Pullquote:** where part of the text is taken from the body copy and reproduced on the same page in a larger, bolder typeface.

**Ragged left/right:** lines of type which are not aligned, or justified, at the left- or right-hand margin.

**Range left/right**: align type on the left or right, so that the other edge is ragged.

**Register:** the exact matching of two or more printings especially when printing more than one color.

**Resolution:** sharpness of definition of a digitized image depending on the number of scan lines to the inch.

**Reverse out:** to print white type or other images on a black background.

**Running head:** heading or title set at the top of each page and separate from the text.

**Saddle stitch:** a type of binding achieved by passing a wire or thread through the center of a folded section.

**Sans serif:** a typeface without serifs.

**Serif**: the small finishing stroke at the end of the main strokes of a letter.

**Side head**: a subhead in, or flush with, the side margin.

**Standfirst:** introduction to article set in a different face from the rest of the text. Purpose is to whet the reader's appetite.

**Stress:** the apparent direction of a letterform given emphasis by the heaviest part of a curved stroke.

**Subhead:** a heading within the body of the text, marking the division of a chapter.

**Tint**: a flat area of dots or lines in a percentage of a main color.

**Typeface**: the image of a letter designed to be made up into words and sentences and printed by some means.

**Typesetting**: text produced by a laserprinter or high quality machine known as a typesetter.

**Typography**: the practice of arranging type.

**Ultra**: the heaviest weight of a particular typeface.

**Unjustified**: text set ranged to the left with the right-hand edge uneven.

**Uppercase**: capital letters

**Vectors:** lines or arcs which plot the outline of a letterform.

**Weight:** the degree of boldness or thickness of a letter or font.

**Widow**: a single word standing as the last line of a paragraph in typeset copy.

**WOB**: white on black (see reverse out).

**Word space**: the space left between words in a line.

**WYSIWYG**: acronym for What You See (on screen) Is What You Get (at the printer).

**x-height**: the height of the lowercase letters in a font, excluding the ascenders and descenders.